THE MACKENZIE CUP

presented on the occasion of the

16th Annual MacKenzie Cup Invitational

April 28, 2009

to

CHASE MARTIN

TOM CROW
KING OF CLUBS

Tom Crow
King of Clubs

Reflections on the game from the course to Cobra

Tom Crow
with Al Barkow

Foreword by Greg Norman

 British American Publishing Ltd.

This publication was initiated and orchestrated by Life^n Press.

2005 British American Publishing, Ltd.

Published by British American Publishing, Ltd.
4 British American Boulevard
Latham, New York 12110
Printed in the United States of America
ISBN 0-945167-56-3

Library of Congress Cataloging-in-Publication Data

Crow, Tom.
Tom Crow, king of clubs / by Tom Crow with Al Barkow.-- 1st ed.
p. cm.
ISBN 0-945167-56-3 (alk. paper)
1. Golf--United States--Equipment and supplies. 2. Golf clubs
(Sporting goods)--United States. 3. Golf equipment industry--
United States. 4. Crow, Tom. I. Barkow, Al. II. Title.

GV976.C76 2004
796.352'028--dc22
2004013856

This book is dedicated to:

My father and mother
whose love and support were always there;

My wife Cally,
my best friend and partner, who raised our
children while I was traipsing around the world;

My brothers, Mac and Peter,
who helped me develop any athletic talent I had;

Clare Higson, my second father;

Bill Johnston,
who taught me the principles of golf club design;

Gary Biszantz,
my white knight and great friend;

My Cobra family and all the PGA professionals,
who were loyal supporters, customers, and friends;

Greg Norman,
who helped make Cobra a household name in golf;

Hale Irwin and John Schroeder,
who also carried the torch;

Lastly, all those too many to name here
who helped me along the way.

Tom Crow

"Golf means fellowship. It bridges the gap of generations. It is the only game I know where a father and his son may meet on exactly an equal basis, where the good player and the duffer may compete on the same terms.

I know I can meet men one hundred times on a business or social footing and never know them. But once you go out on the golf course with a man and play the game with him, you know him.

Golf to me has meant and always will mean a list of real friendships besides which all other successes of life are negligible. Of course, it's a great thing in my life. But the greatest thing in golf is friendship."

~ BOBBY JONES *circa 1930*

FOREWORD

Tom Crow has done a tremendous amount for the game we all love. He is passionate about golf, he enjoys the people, he loves the business, and he is a genius at building golf clubs.

Early in life Tom had considerable success as an amateur golfer. He won the Australian Amateur in 1961 and represented Australia in The Eisenhower Cup and the St. Andrews Matches during the same era. But then his entrepreneurial flare took over and he went on to success of even broader scope.

Tom's new career took off when he joined Precision Golf Forging in Sydney, where he gained a sophisticated understanding of how and why a golf club works. This valuable experience led directly to the most important decision in his life: at forty-two, Tom decided to move from Australia to the United States and have a go with club design on his own. The result was Cobra Golf, founded in 1973.

For Tom, golf was always a personal business and so Cobra was very much a family company. He quickly established relationships with golf professionals and he acknowledges that this was one of the early catalysts for Cobra's success. Perhaps most important, Cobra did not try to follow others in design. Cobra was a pioneer, always on the cutting edge. Yet all the while, it remained a grassroots organization.

Today, Tom Crow has been involved in golf club design for more than thirty years. His experience and ingenuity are shown by many innovations in the golf equipment market: the three-wedge system, the first extra-length driver—dubbed the "Long Tom"—and the reintroduction of graphite shafts for lighter-weight clubs in the mid 1980s. He developed the Baffler in 1975, which set the utility-wood standard in the golf industry. Variations of the Baffler have been made and sold by virtually every major golf manufacturer. The King Cobra line of oversized woods and irons are further examples of his design expertise, and they are among the best sellers in industry history.

Overall, I'd say Tom Crow was probably twenty-five years ahead of his time. This made me all the more pleased when he told me one day that a key step in Cobra's success came as a result of a phone call I made to him in the late 1970s. I had called and asked for a set of Cobra clubs. About ten weeks later I called again and asked for a backup set. Tom asked me if the first set was okay. I remember telling him, "Yes, I think the first set was all right. I won four tournaments in seven weeks with them!" From that point our friendship grew and in 1988 I became personally involved with Cobra by acquiring 12 percent of the company. So I have been in the fortunate position of working closely with Tom and seeing Cobra grow to the stature it did as one of golf's dominant club manufacturers.

Tom stands among those leaders in the golf industry

who believe in focusing solely on products of the very highest standard. Through his long commitment to excellence and service to golf, he has had a positive impact on the development of the game and the livelihood of many golfers around the world.

Tom has always said that it is relatively easy to make clubs for a great player, but quite another matter to make clubs for players who are less skilled. He knew that if you could make equipment that would help someone improve from a score of 100 down to 90, you would have a really valuable effect on the game. Tom was proud to be part of the effort to have that kind of effect and therefore to make the game more enjoyable for greater numbers of everyday golfers.

In January 2004, Tom received The Ernie Sabayrac Award from the PGA of America, for lifetime contributions to golf. It is their most prestigious award and a fitting climax to an extraordinary career.

As the success of Cobra Golf makes clear, Tom Crow is rightly considered one of the premier golf equipment designers in the world. His legacy will stand the test of time and his impact will be felt for years to come. Tom is one of the more influential people in my own life, and I am proud to have him as a close friend and confidant.

Greg Norman

PREFACE

Interestingly, the idea of asking Tom Crow to write a book of his stories and insights on the game of golf began because of another amateur golfer, Bobby Jones, and the efforts of the people who worked to bring Jones' life to film.

Tom was instrumental in the making of that tribute to Jones' legacy, the award-winning motion picture, *Bobby Jones-Stroke of Genius*. Producing a film often creates a fraternity of friends. Some say this is because of the intense stress and strain of filmmaking (not unlike the bonds of war); others say it is because of the memorable adventures that are shared. In our case, it was a bit of both.

For all of us involved, Tom Crow was an inspiring and ever-challenging voice through the entire journey from script to film. Bobby Jones is one of his heroes. And as one aspect of his lifework legacy in the sport, Tom was keen to tell "the story behind the story" of Mr. Jones.

When you read this book and watch *Stroke of Genius*, you will understand why. One cannot mistake the influence of Jones in Tom's own story. Bobby Jones personified the ethic of the amateur code, he was one of the sport's great entrepreneurs, and he was passionate about the fellowship of the game. All of these are essential elements of Tom's perspective and experiences.

Indeed, the two shared many sentiments, as well as interests. They are two remarkable men in the game of golf and the game of life. They have hit the ball straight and true, and inspire us to do the same.

Life^n Press
Rick Eldridge, Paul Brooks,
Bob Keys, Jim Van Eerden
& The Legacy Partners of Robert Tyre Jones, Jr.

CONTENTS

INTRODUCTION

I saw a bumper sticker not long ago which read, "Life's a game. But Golf is serious." For me, the great and serious game of golf has brought extraordinary opportunities, remarkable good fortune, wonderful people, and lasting friendships.

Preparing to write this brief story of my golfing life has helped me recognize key moments that have shaped me and to remember vividly the people with whom I shared them. It's a story of uprooting and making a home in a new country, of having the good luck to participate in golf's exploding popularity across America and the world, of meeting and learning from remarkable individuals, and of providing for my own loving family while building a new family in the worlds of golf and business.

Modern executives, especially those of us who have managed a degree of success, like to imagine that we hold at least a little sway over the world around us and our own destinies. Of course, we give ourselves too much credit. Our lives, like everyone's, are full of events both great and small that can turn out to be life-changing, though we may not even recognize these turning points while we are experiencing them. There have been many such events in my life, which saw a generally unremarkable Australian lad from an ordinary family find his fortune an ocean away in southern California. One day I was a high school student with a football injury, whiling away my time learning the game of golf. Four decades later, I had founded a major company manufacturing golf equipment.

For having been able to undertake this fortunate and exciting journey, I feel both gratitude and humility. I hope that my reflections here may have interest for those who love, as I do, the great and serious game of golf.

PART I

THIS ANCIENT YET EVER YOUNG SPORT

1

LIVELY BALLS
AND HOT DRIVERS

It has been my great good fortune that my life's work—my involvement in the golf equipment industry—has coincided with an era of significant change in the field. You could call it a revolution. In my own small way, I believe I helped that revolution along, and this has been an exciting and challenging experience.

In the past three decades especially, there have been extraordinary developments, first in the materials that are the basis for golf equipment, and then in the construction and design concepts that these materials have made possible. Golf has come to be played in a new way as equipment advances and other developments have made the game more readily playable for more people.

Paralleling the improvements in equipment have been similar improvements in the conditioning and maintenance of golf courses over the last half-century. An old pro, when asked about the major changes in the game he'd observed since his youth, responded tellingly, "The lawnmower." New strains of grasses, sophisticated drainage techniques, and, even better lawnmowers have had almost as much impact on the game as graphite and titanium. Some of the improvements may also have brought unintended complications, but I'll get to that shortly.

I am grateful, and also proud, to have been a part of what I believe to be real progress in the game of golf. I'm convinced that most of the changes in the game have been for the better—although that view is not universal!

Vigorous arguments have been made in recent

years concerning the technological advances in golf equipment. The majority of these comments have come out of the game's two main governing bodies, the United States Golf Association (USGA) and the Royal & Ancient Golf Club of St. Andrews (R&A), which are the keepers of the game and its traditions. Some blame for what they deem to be negative consequences for golf has been laid at the feet of the golf equipment manufacturers and there is some credibility for that view.

There is concern that technology is taking the place of skill as the most important factor. One claim, for example, is that the new balls, especially when hit with the new types of drivers, travel too far and with less deviation. With the new equipment adding so much length to the games of even high-handicappers, so the thinking goes, the great classic courses that are at the heart of golf's rich traditions are becoming too short to be challenging, and are on their way to becoming obsolete.

I grew up in the game of golf, and have always maintained a deep connection to it and an abiding respect for its traditions. I don't believe that I, or my colleagues and competitors in the golf industry, have betrayed those traditions.

It is easy to say—and in fact it is quite true—that equipment manufacturers only make and sell what the market desires, and in fact demands. After all, it's not the golfers themselves who object to balls that explode off the clubface or to clubs that are easier to hit with. In my experience we've never had a customer send back a club because it hit the ball too far or too straight.

The handicap of the average golfer over the last thirty-five years, roughly the era of rapid technological advance in golf, has remained virtually the same. If all those millions of golfers using the latest *high-tech* balls and *hot* drivers were consistently shooting lower scores, then the arguments raised against modern equipment might hold some water. But the records show that, in fact, average golfers are not consistently shooting lower scores than their predecessors on courses around the world. Doesn't this mean that the integrity of the game has actually not been weakened at all?

I look at things this way: Whether or not golfers may be scoring better with the graphite shafts, metal heads, perimeter-weighted clubs, and aerodynamically miraculous balls, there's no question that the average golfer is enjoying the game more. There's less shock and vibration to the hands when the ball is mishit, slices and hooks happen less often or are less severe, the ball is lofted more easily and consistently, and the balls last a good deal longer. Isn't all that worth quite a lot?

However, having said that, I am on the side of the USGA and the R&A which have to make the rules for the playing of the game. The manufacturers must accept, from time to time, rule changes, and conform to those changes.

Remember when there was no limit on the number of clubs a player could carry? Some professionals had over twenty clubs in the bag until a limit of fourteen was established.

The modern reaction to attempts to modify the rules are threats of lawsuits by the offending manufacturer. I disagree strongly with that attitude.

There should be rules which maintain the essence of the game as it developed, as well as guidelines for bringing the game into the twenty-first century.

2

THE LONG AND SHORT OF IT

One is tempted to wonder if the USGA and the R&A would like to see the game return to its early beginnings, with everyone playing with hickory-shafted clubs and gutta-percha balls. However, history tells us that even the Scots, who brought this game into being centuries ago, never stopped trying to improve their equipment. They were always coming up with ways to make a livelier ball, or a club that hit the ball farther and straighter with less effort. They even designed a range of special clubs for different kinds of trouble shots, and we use some of them today.

In my own lifetime, I can point to the example of Bobby Jones, a man who inspired me greatly and who was himself a strong believer in golf tradition, as his famous Masters tournament reflects. Jones won all his championships with hickory-shafted clubs. Yet when Spalding brought out the company's first steel-shafted irons in 1930, Jones put his name on them. He saw the future and he didn't flinch. It's interesting to note that a few years before that, when steel shafts were initially introduced, neither the USGA nor the R&A would approve them. It took the USGA three years to come around on that issue, and the R&A a bit longer.

I don't actually believe the USGA or R&A really wants to take golf back in time a couple of centuries, or deny golfers the genuine advancements in equipment that have come about in recent years. They do have a legitimate concern, and that is the need to place some kind of limits on the equipment the pros are using on the tournament circuits. Here I think the only real cause for alarm is hitting distance—though even in that regard, the governing bodies may be overreacting. It's proven every week on the pro tour that the longest hitter is not the guaranteed winner. John Daly, for instance, is one of the game's longest hitters, but over a nine-year period, from 1996 to 2004, he was able to win only one tournament on the American PGA Tour, and he did that with a marvelous short game. Tiger Woods is a long hitter, and even he doesn't win every tournament he enters. The players who are consistently at the top of the list in driving statistics are not at the top of the winner's list. In other words, distance is nice, but it doesn't make you a consistent winner or champion. It's only one of the elements of a winning game, and perhaps one of the lesser ones.

I recall when the issue of equipment technology seemed to reach a crisis point in 1998. The day before that year's U.S. Open, the USGA held a press conference. The CEOs of all the leading equipment makers were there, as were the media and other interested observers The press conference was touted in advance as a big deal. David Fay, the executive secretary of the USGA, fielded questions. When pushed, he at last admitted that the only real problem the association had in regard to equipment was that the players were hitting the ball too far.

That said, a few days later Lee Janzen won the U.S. Open—and Lee was a medium-length hitter.

There has been talk of establishing two separate sets of rules governing equipment, one for the tournament pros and one for the rest of the world's amateur and recreational golfers. I disagree emphatically with this idea, and here's an illustration for my reasons: Check out Torrey Pines Golf Course in San Diego on the Monday after the San Diego Open has just been played there. On that day, Torrey Pines gets one of its biggest crowds of the year because everybody wants to test themselves playing from the same tees and to the same pin positions as the pros did.

Everyday golfers want the truest possible experience, challenging and measuring themselves with the same basic equipment the pros use. To deny them that opportunity would be to destroy another of golf's unique and beloved traditions. A baseball fan can never stand in the batter's box at Yankee Stadium and face a major-league fastball, but any golfer can see how he or she stacks up on the same holes that Jack Nicklaus or Tiger Woods or Karrie Webb or Se Ri Pak has played just the day before.

My thought is that the USGA and R&A should make and enforce the rules of the game, but perhaps the rules that govern equipment should be the province of an independent body, including representatives from the USGA and R&A, the equipment manufacturers, and the professional tours. With their shared interests I believe these representatives would never allow the game to be affected by disadvantageous innovations. Could that be a solution to this difficult problem? It's worth some thought.

3

The Ping Eye II
Controversy

Many will remember the outcry when Karsten Solheim brought out the Ping Eye II irons with square grooves in the face. Lost-wax casting, used in the Ping Eye II, produces a groove that is square at the bottom and sharply edged or angled at the face, as opposed to the conventional V-shaped grooves on forged clubs.

There was widespread concern that the square grooves on the Ping Eye II made it too easy to impart spin on the golf ball, allowing the player to control the ball's flight more effectively and ensure that it stopped quickly after landing. That much is true; the Ping Eye does provide those advantages, but *only* when the ball is played out of long and, specifically, *wet* grass. It doesn't offer the same advantages on shots out of short wet grass, or out of dry grass of any length. Yet even notable players, including Jack Nicklaus and Tom Watson, spoke about the groove's effectiveness under all conditions.

The square-groove controversy continued to rage and it became evident that the sharp edges of the groove, on Ping Eye II irons were badly scraping the covers of balls. The tour pros using those clubs were going through at least a half-dozen or more balls each round. Titleist, whose balls were used by a large number of pros, complained that the two dozen balls it provided to these tour players every week weren't enough, but they weren't about to start giving out more to them.

Solheim then responded by having the edges of the grooves beveled to soften them, but the result was that now the space between the grooves, if measured edge to edge *on the surface* of the clubface, was deemed too narrow by the USGA, which maintained that this change made these irons nonconforming.

Solheim sued, concerned that the irons could not be corrected by recalling them, thus forcing thousands of customers to abandon the clubs if they wanted to play by the rules. He knew this result would cost him much goodwill, not to mention millions of dollars. Both parties firmly stood their ground and their arguments went before a judge in Phoenix. In the end, the USGA, with the president of the association casting the deciding vote, agreed to grandfather the Ping Eye II irons. All those already in play on the pro tours, the amateur circuits, and of course in recreational golf, would for all time be deemed exempt and therefore legal.

The R&A felt differently. That body outlawed the Ping Eye II irons. Since the R&A was not part of the lawsuit against the USGA, Solheim would have had to face them separately in a British court. He chose not to, and instead agreed to revise the grooves and the spaces between them on any and all irons he produced subsequent to the clubs being grandfathered.

I agreed with the USGA position, but not with their decision to grandfather. I think the R&A got this one right. Interestingly, though, in the most thorough research to date on the science of golf equipment, *The Search for the Perfect Swing*, authors Alastair Cochran and John Stobbs assert that the grooves on irons actually have little or no effect on the amount of spin imparted to the ball. Rather, it is the angle of the club's attack that determines spin. Yet this matter has generated a great deal of angst and has cost people a lot of money.

All the more reason, I think, to leave these decisions up to the pros and those who administer the tours. I believe they would sensibly monitor the equipment used in competition and bar any that provide unfair performance capabilities. Of course, as I have said, the USGA and R&A should not be left out of the equation, nor should the equipment manufacturers.

4

SOME MODEST
PROPOSALS

An interesting feature of the contemporary golf scene is that there is no standard length for any club. For many years, drivers were all 43.5 inches long. Now, however, most are at least 45 inches. The longer the club, the wider the swing arc and so the greater the swing velocity. Since club length has little to do with a golfer's height, condition, or ability, I suggest standardizing the length of the longest club to 45 inches.

In the same vein, I would suggest ensuring that the putter be the shortest club in the bag, as it traditionally was. Golfers now use extra-long putters and can create a point of balance and control by pressing the butt end of the club up against their body or chin, almost like a fulcrum. I think that negates one of golf's basic skill factors, the ability to control the club with the hands.

I would also make some changes to our golf courses that would tend to bring basic skill factors back into use. Golfers have all become used to, perhaps dependent on, yardage markers on the courses, pin sheets that give precise pin placements, and new space-age devices on the carts that display all this information at the touch of a button. These conveniences are all intended to speed up play by making it no longer necessary to pace off yardages and so on. But the fact is that since their advent, the length of the average round has increased to somewhere between five and five-and-a-half hours. Who knows, perhaps without all the pin sheets to pore over, and without golfers scouring the fairways for sprinkler heads and markers, the pace might pick up a little. In any case, eliminating these artificial aids would require golfers to develop their natural visual judgment.

And then there's the Stimpfmeter. I remember the disdain of the superintendent of the legendary Muirfield Golf Club in Scotland when he was told that the device measures the speed of a green. "What do we need that for?" he asked. When told that it was used to make the greens consistent, he scoffed, "It's up to the players to find that out," and rejected the meter.

About balls: while I recognize that all other ball sports use a standardized ball, I don't believe there should be a universal ball in use on the tournament circuits. Golf is an extremely individual game. Golfers use the clubs of their choice, and should be able to use the ball that best suits their game.

For many years in the history of golf, up until the early 1970s, there was a size difference between the balls used in America and those used in Britain. The difference was not great—a diameter of 1.62 inches for the British ball compared to 1.68 for the American. That's only four one-hundredths of an inch. The two balls weighed the same and it was true that the smaller British ball traveled somewhat further, especially when played into the wind and with curve in cross winds.

That it played better in the wind was the British ball's main advantage, and it made sense to use it in Great Britain, where the seaside links and even the inland courses are subject to wind, sometimes quite strong wind a great deal of the time. The smaller ball was less apt to float when hit into the wind, and would maintain that desired low, boring trajectory more easily than the bigger ball. It was also somewhat less vulnerable to crosswinds.

Interestingly, because the bigger ball was harder to play under windy conditions, the British tour professionals decided one day to make it mandatory on their tournament circuit. This was one of those odd paradoxes common in the world of golf. The British professional golfing community members felt that they were dominated by the Americans, especially in the Ryder Cup matches. In fact, the Americans had so dominated the Ryder Cup that there was even talk of discontinuing the matches for lack of competition.

The British thought that since the American ball was harder to play on their usually windy courses, learning how to manipulate it effectively would force them all to become better players, making the international competition more balanced.

In 1968 the bigger ball was put into play on the European tournament circuit, and by 1970 Tony Jacklin was able to win the U.S. Open, becoming the first native Briton to do so in forty-nine years. Jacklin managed to get out to a good lead after an opening round of 71 in a 45-mile-per-hour wind on the Hazeltine Golf Course in Minnesota. Ironically, the American superstars Jack Nicklaus and Arnold Palmer scored 81 and 79 respectively on that day. The bigger ball became the international standard, making the smaller British ball a relic of the past.

Some players, including the outstanding Australian golfer Peter Thomson, continued to defend the smaller ball. Thomson won five British Opens using the smaller ball, not to mention many other events throughout Europe, Asia, and Australia. However when he came to

America to play the Senior PGA Tour in 1985, he won nine events and was that tour's leading money winner for the season playing with the larger ball.

However, I do support maintaining the current limit on the speed at which the ball leaves the club face: 150 feet per second. The rule now allows a margin for error of plus 1 percent. That 1 percent adds approximately 12 yards to the drive when hit at 110 miles per hour, the average swing speed among tour pros. While the rule is sound as it is now written, I'd recommend eliminating the plus-1 margin for error.

Another thought of mine is that the officials on the various tours and at the Open championships do on-site testing of the balls that players will use in competition to ensure that they conform to regulations. I wouldn't be surprised if some might be found at first to be over the limit, in terms of feet-per-second velocity. The Japanese tour star, Jumbo Ozaki, may serve as an example. He and Greg Norman drive the ball the same distance when they both play in American tournaments, but in Japan Greg has found himself as much as 40 yards behind Ozaki off the tee. Perhaps the Japanese are not as strict as the Americans about checking ball velocity standards.

5

OF GREENS
AND BROWN

There is one simple way to quiet the furor over equipment: rethink course conditioning and course setup. Make the courses firmer and therefore faster running. Tighten the fairways and increase the length of the rough.

This comment is meant especially for American golf. Americans have become accustomed to soft, lush, green golf courses, which are in no small part responsible for the rise of the new high-tech equipment. In the harsher landscape of Scotland where golf was born, and throughout much of the world, golf has always been played both in the air and *on the ground*. But the conditions in America have changed the way it is played here and have made the new equipment desirable, if not downright necessary.

I liken American golf to the game of darts. Pinpoint accuracy and distance through the air have taken precedence over reading the landscape and managing the roll of the ball after it lands. When the fairways and greens are so lush and cushiony, all shots must be played to carry as far as possible and to stop almost immediately upon landing, at least around the greens. Equipment has been designed to fulfill these needs. Perimeter-weighted metal drivers are intended to get the ball into the air so it carries as far as possible. Perimeter-weighted irons are designed with the same purpose in mind—essentially shooting darts.

Many point to Augusta National Golf Club and its presentation of the Masters tournament as setting the standard for golf course conditioning. Members of American clubs look to Augusta and demand that their own courses exhibit the same vivid green, the same carpeted feel. Of course, Augusta National spends an enormous amount of money to keep the course looking so rich and pristine, but with all due respect to my many friends there, it's possible that they may have unwittingly done a disservice to the game.

One of the game's most successful players on the great American courses, Jack Nicklaus, also won more than his share on British-style courses because of his extraordinary talent and game-management skills. But the style of play required in Britain didn't come naturally to Jack.

In his first year on the PGA Tour, he had to play some of the public-fee courses, such as the heavily used Rancho Park in Los Angeles. Having grown up on a superbly conditioned private course, Scioto Golf Club, Jack was probably less than thrilled about playing Rancho Park, where the greens were neither smooth nor soft and where, significantly, the par-5s were relatively short. Some observers have mused that in those early years Jack may have avoided courses where his competitors had a good chance of reaching the par-5s in two shots. Jack's length was his strength, which is to say that part of his competitive advantage rested on his being able to reach par-5s that were unreachable for his competitors. Jack's length off the tee and in the air was prodigious, and given that he could hit his 1-iron as high as other pros hit their 7-irons, lush green courses suited his game perfectly. He was a master of darts.

It is noted that when Jack played his first Los Angeles Open at Rancho Park he earned the princely sum of $16.50.

The overly luxuriant—in my view—state of American golf courses seems to be a case of best intentions gone awry. The Greens Committee of the USGA has done wonderful research and development and overseen great strides in the care and feeding of golf course grass. As a result, it's become far easier than ever before to produce and maintain luxuriant green golf courses— and as I've said, equipment has evolved to suit these courses.

It will probably come as no surprise to the reader when I suggest that the solution is to return to drier courses. Without rain, drier courses are tan or dull yellow-brown. When the rains come, the courses are softer and greener, but only until they dry out, a process that can be abetted by a well-designed drainage system. Today's sophisticated irrigation systems, now used to keep the courses consistently well-nourished, should really only be used to protect the grass against dying during extremely dry periods. I believe this drier-course approach would bring the game closer to its elemental origins, a somewhat purer game pitting man against nature. Some days you'll have to shoot darts, but other days you'll have to play the roll.

On the overwatered courses we've all become used to, the game never changes. The same shots are required day in, day out, from season to season. I truly believe that every golfer's experience will be enriched if Americans let go of their demands for permanently lush green courses. It would signal the end of all the arguments about how hot balls have become, how thin the face of a driver is, or whatever other technological development is the issue of the day.

I've gotten involved on an advisory basis with the American Golf Course Superintendents Association. One of our goals is to make people aware that green is not necessarily beautiful. Green is really only a by-product of the overwatering that has made our courses too soft. The greener our courses become, the further we get from the game as it's been played for hundreds of years in Scotland, in Australia, and indeed in America up until the 1940s.

Maintenance would also be simpler and perhaps less stressful. Firmer greens are less vulnerable to damage from soft cleats and metal spikes. They will stay smoother longer with less investment of time and money in close-cutting and rolling.

Green doesn't necessarily indicate a healthy course, either. Claude Crockford, or "Crocky," the wonderful greens superintendent at Royal Melbourne, said this about the watering of courses: "Grass is just like human beings. Overfeed it and overwater it and it becomes fat and lazy and susceptible to disease. Just underfeed it and under-water it and it becomes strong and virile." That's a valuable analogy. I think the USGA could do a great service to the game by discouraging overwatering and promoting "brown is beautiful." There could be a larger benefit to such an effort, given the water shortages that afflict parts of this country. Already some courses are using recycled water, a trend that's likely to grow.

Old Crocky was masterful when it came to greens. Every year he lifted six of the thirty-six greens at Royal

Melbourne, cutting them into 15-inch squares and putting them through a sod cutter to remove the root structure and thatch that had accumulated over time. Then he would lay the grass back down to the exact topography. But here's the thing: he marked every square of grass he had taken up so that he knew exactly where it had come from on the green, and in the process of replacing them, changed the location of every piece. A piece from the northeast section would now go into the southwest section, and so on. The same topography would remain—but every seven years there would be a whole new set of greens.

Crocky also had something to say about undulation on greens. In my opinion, some of today's course architects are too radical in the way they design and build their greens—the mounding and reversals of cant are enough to make golfers dizzy. But the greens built a generation or two ago by legendary architects such as A.W. Tillinghast, Alister MacKenzie, and Donald Ross were basically tilted down from back to front. The idea was that when it rained, the greens would drain naturally to the front and thus stay relatively dry.

This canting of the older putting surfaces also had ramifications for strategy and course management. Hit your approach shot above the hole and you're facing a tough down-hiller. Land it on either side of the hole and you've got to worry about the break from right to left or left to right. The best place to be is below the hole so you can putt straight uphill, meaning that golfers have to develop good control of their shot-making.

The only hole at Pebble Beach where the green tilts

down from front to back is the fifth that was put in a few years ago. To my way of thinking, it's all wrong for the shot into it, which is of some length. You could hit as crisp an iron shot as you can imagine, and your ball still might not hold the green.

We shouldn't have to trick up the greens with the roller-coaster hills and dales that are so popular with today's golf course architects, especially when most greens play so fast. It isn't that it's unfair to provide these questionable amenities, but rather that doing so fails to reward smart shot-making into the green. I feel the same way about the artificial bumps and hummocks out on the course. Crocky used to say that the only way to make these seem a natural part of the terrain was to make sure that the width at the base was ten times the height of the rise. That isn't always the case these days.

If the USGA wants to prevent the game's best players from bringing our best golf courses to their knees, they must never forget that dry, fast-running courses will always be more challenging and dangerous than soft, lush ones. Think back to the 2003 British Open, played at St. George's, a difficult course because of the high bounces and the speed of the ground. It isn't a long course, but the conditioning made it extremely dangerous. The USGA does make an effort to condition its U.S. Open courses in the same fashion, but the tournament is always played in June, after spring rains. If the courses were designed and conditioned so that water is absorbed or drained quickly, they would have a better chance of staying firm and fast, and the U.S. Open would be a far more interesting event every year.

Counterintuitive though it may seem, lengthening courses isn't the way to make the game more challenging for top players. If you let the players shoot darts, driving to soft fairways and approaching to soft greens, you can make a course 8,000 yards long and it still won't beat these players.

We should think instead about standardizing the length of the grass on the fringe areas around the greens, so that an approach that is slightly off the mark will run away from the green. The USGA feels that thickly grassed fringes are more demanding, but I don't agree. To illustrate this point, we can look back some twenty years to a U.S. Open played at Baltusrol, where the fringes around the greens were three to four inches thick. The fringes had never been allowed to grow that high before, but with the new wedges with fifty-eight or sixty degrees of loft, shots out of that heavy grass were no longer a problem. I remember the winner that year, Lee Janzen, just missing the green with a 180-yard approach shot, and before he even started walking up the fairway he was reaching for his sixty-degree wedge. He already knew exactly the kind of shot he was going to play. This doesn't really speak well for the course.

By contrast, when the fringes were mowed close at Pinehurst No. 2 for the 1990 U.S. Open, as they always are at Augusta National for the Masters, a golfer who was just off the green was faced with a variety of options. He could pitch it, chip it, or putt from the fringe, and any of those shots would require considerably more skill than what amounts to a basic sand shot out of thick fringe. That year, the course played a relatively short 6,900 yards, but it was still a legitimate test of skill. Payne Stewart won it with a 279, only eight shots under par.

Some will say that the recreational golfer with average skills would rather play out of lush grass than go back to fast, brown courses. Many people think it's easier to get the ball in the air from a cushy lie, but this isn't actually true. If average golfers would learn to hit the ball from firmer lies, this would quickly improve their game overall. On top of that, they'd have the advantage of much more roll in the fairways, even on poorly hit shots—a particular boon to senior golfers who may not be able to carry the ball as far as they once could. No thin-walled driver with a miraculous trampoline effect or hot high-tech ball is going to provide the same advantage.

For years people have talked about how long Bobby Jones was off the tee, at a time when he played with hickory-shafted clubs and pure balata golf balls. But they forget that he was also playing in an era when courses were not watered as they are now; he got a lot of his yardage, as did everyone else, from roll.

Perhaps it appears that my views on course conditioning are somewhat contradictory to my general support for technological innovation in equipment. Or maybe I sound too much like a dyed-in-the-wool traditionalist about the way golf used to be. The truth is that nothing is ever black and white, that the most successful developments in any field arise out of reasonable compromise, out of finding sensible middle ground. I believe that in the game of golf there is no reason why modern science and technology can't co-exist with a respect for the natural landscape as it relates to the ancient traditions and highest skills of golf.

6

GREATNESS

When you've been around golf as long as I have, you can't avoid being asked your opinions about the greatest players in the game. I don't mind tackling the question, with the caveat that it's surely impossible to single out one person as the best of all time.

It's hard to compare golfers from different eras, given the evolution of equipment and the changes in course conditioning, not to mention a host of cultural and commercial considerations. However, human nature doesn't change all that much, and on that basis I have to believe that a player with Ben Hogan's fierce will to win, Jack Nicklaus' self-control, and Peter Thomson's brilliant mind for the game would have been great in any time and place, whether it was a hayfield in the 1920s with hickory-shafted clubs and gutta-percha balls or an immaculately groomed garden with the space-age equipment of the twenty-first century.

And you can't spend very much time in golf without hearing something about Bobby Jones, so important is he to the history of the game. As a youngster, I had heard the name of course, but hadn't taken the time to learn much about Jones' story. Later, when I spent time traveling around America and Europe as an assistant to Peter Thomson, I began to learn about Bobby Jones in greater depth. Peter would talk a lot to me about Jones, not just about his phenomenal record as a golfer, but about his character. I hadn't realized that Jones actually played relatively little golf throughout the year. He played only in the summer, whether for pleasure or in competition. Given his special genius for the game, he didn't put in long hours beating balls on the practice range. His schedule was that of a true amateur—*amateur* in the most literal sense of the word, in that he played because he loved it.

There was an old joke that Jones won all his championships while generally playing no more golf than the average doctor. A truly amazing fact of Jones' career, which has now become legend, is that after his crowning achievement of winning the Grand Slam, that is, the four major titles of his day in one year—the United States and British Open and Amateur championships—he retired from competitive golf. *At the age of 28.*

It took me awhile to appreciate what was behind Jones' decision. As a young person, I couldn't understand why someone would quit at the absolute height of his ability, with so much more that might be accomplished. Slowly, though, I learned about Jones' commitment to his family and his community and the seriousness with which he approached his career. I also came to understand that Jones was a very cerebral man, a man who thought deeply and carefully about his life and who ended up putting a lot of pressure on himself. The stress of competition caused a great deal of inner turmoil for Jones. Such factors surely must have entered into his decision.

Jones was a man of honor, as demonstrated in a story about him that has been passed down for years. While preparing to play a shot during a tournament, he accidentally moved his ball an imperceptible fraction of an inch. No one even saw the ball move, yet Jones called a penalty on himself. When commended on his decision,

Jones famously commented that to congratulate him for the calling the stroke on himself was like congratulating him for not robbing a bank.

I had the great pleasure of meeting Bobby Jones once, at the 1958 Masters. I only spent a few moments with him, but could clearly see all the qualities that made him who he was, and made such an impression on me: warmth, intelligence, great integrity, and an expansive and generous worldview.

As for the greatness of legends such as Gene Sarazen and Walter Hagen, I'm satisfied to take the word of those who actually saw them play. Their records alone tell us all we need to know. What I want to focus on here are the players I observed with my own eyes. Of these, I'd say that Ben Hogan was at least the second-best player I ever saw. I watched him only once, in one of the smaller events on the pro tour, but the impact on me was considerable.

While I was traveling in the U.S. with Peter Thomson, I asked him if I could take a day off to watch Ben Hogan. Hogan was playing at Seminole Golf Club in Florida, where he always went in late winter or early spring to prepare for the Masters. Seminole was ideal because, like Augusta National, it requires precision ball control, and it was that control which impressed me most about Hogan. I watched him play thirty-six holes that day. He hit every fairway and every green in regulation including all the par 5s in 2. But this was already 1958, the first year he would miss the cut in the Masters, and by then his putting was getting twitchy. For all that marvelous ball striking at Seminole, he had thirty-six putts in the first round and thirty-seven in the second. But I will never forget the way he controlled the ball flight of all his shots from tee to green.

The eighth hole at Seminole is a 235-yard par 3, a giant of a hole, at least in those days. Hogan was paired with Mike Souchak, a long-ball hitter, who used a 3-wood and put the ball in the front middle of the green. The pin was in the back right corner. Hogan used a driver and hit an exquisite little cut shot that landed on the left half of the green, ran toward the hole, and stopped within 12 feet. In the afternoon he hit an almost identical shot, and he made three both times.

Peter Thomson—about whom I'll have more to say in a later chapter—ranks high on my list of great players. I had a chance to see his greatness in action many times, but one event stands out particularly. This was the 1958 British Open, played at Royal Lytham.

In those days, every player was required to qualify, even the defending champion, in this case Bobby Locke, to whom Peter had been runner-up the previous year. Peter qualified on the Royal Lytham course, and I did so nearby at St. Anne's. We were staying at the St. Anne's Hotel, which was also housing the elite golf writers of the day—Peter Ryde, Pat Ward-Thomas, Leonard Crawley, Henry Longhurst, and others. That week Peter had been having a lot of trouble with hay fever and at times it seemed his medications were making things worse, since he had developed a terrible rash from an antihistamine injection. The night before his qualifying round, he had been unable to sleep, and so we spent that night sitting around with a group of these writers.

In the course of conversation, Henry Longhurst asked Peter what he thought the modern professional golfer was capable of achieving, how well he might play. Many years later, I still remember Peter's answer clearly. "Well, that's a very subjective question," he said. "The best answer I can give is, if the wind is less than 10 miles per hour and the fairways are firm, I think the best modern professionals have the capacity to hit the ball on the correct side of the fairway off the tee and to within 20 feet of the hole with their approach to every green. Perhaps one day I'll be able to demonstrate that."

That day came the very next morning, which broke clear and calm. The course was firm as well, creating the very conditions Peter had outlined. He had an 8:30 A.M. tee time and as I was not set to go off until that afternoon, I walked the course with him during his round. So did Leonard Crawley, which was remarkable in itself. Crawley was notorious for never walking the course to cover a tournament. Peter played flawlessly. At the ninth green, he barely missed a putt of some 6 feet that would have given him a 29 for the front. He hit the flagstick twice with his approaches, and while he didn't come within 10 feet of the hole on every approach, as he had predicted, his only two longer putts were 30 and 45 feet for a final score of 63.

Crawley stayed for the entire round, and the next day wrote one of those beautiful pieces of his about having seen a great modern professional performing at the peak of his ability. Peter won his fourth Open that year, in a playoff with Dave Thomas.

It's interesting to compare Peter Thomson's game to

that of Byron Nelson, another beautiful golfer. Peter had a round-ish swing, whereas Nelson's was very upright, perhaps the first player of the modern era to swing the club more vertically, rather than around his body. Nelson's swing path was relatively straight up and straight down, with no rerouting, demonstrating the law of physics that every action has an equal and opposite reaction.

I believe Peter Thomson thought that Sam Snead was the most talented golfer he had ever seen. Snead was a fantastic player who could hit any type of shot. It's a shame that he was never able to win a U.S. Open, a void in his record shaped by exceptionally poor play on the last hole of the 1939 championship, in Philadelphia. Snead thought he needed a birdie 4 on the last hole and tried a risky shot that didn't work out. He made 8 and ended up missing a playoff for the title by 2 strokes.

I have always admired Lloyd Mangrum, also because of his terrific ball control. That control may have resulted from his standing over the ball with his feet only about a foot apart, even with the driver. He had an interesting, almost military manner, with very erect posture and very slow and methodical motions. Even his backswing was slow. I remember a time when he needed a birdie 4 on the last hole to win a tournament, and put his second shot into a greenside bunker. He walked into the bunker casually but purposefully, hit the shot to within a few inches of the cup, and sank the putt to win. When asked if he had felt any pressure, he responded that it was just like going to the office—he did it every day. Mangrum may not have had one of the top records of all time, although he did win a U.S. Open and many tour events, but he was a great player according to my definition.

Of the British players who were more or less my contemporaries, I thought Peter Alliss was a great player. He was a big man who hit beautiful shots, although his putting never quite matched his ball-striking.

All the British golfers of my time, the 1950s and 1960s, played differently than their young countrymen do now. They used the smaller ball and had to play both in the air and along the ground. As a result, they tended to trap the ball, keeping the clubface somewhat closed at impact. Hardly any of today's golfers, regardless of where they're from, play that way anymore. Nowadays, the boys just get behind the ball and lift it high in the air. "Grip it and rip it," as the saying goes. Greg Norman was the first Australian to play that way. David Graham was another terrific player, much underrated. Back in Australia he was called "The Dog" because when he came close to home and had a chance to win, he wouldn't let go. A very tough competitor.

When I said earlier that Ben Hogan may have been the second best player I had seen, I meant second to Jack Nicklaus. Jack was, for some twenty years, the best putter the game had ever produced. Under pressure from inside 12 feet, he was peerless. I've been told by statistically minded people that Jack never missed a putt on the seventy-second hole if he needed it to tie or win, and I can believe it. Hogan made his share of putts—you don't win all those titles without being able to hole out—but it wasn't a strength for him the way it was for Nicklaus. It's what sets Jack above the rest.

Jack also had exceptional self-control on the course, emotionally and otherwise. He never showed anger when something went wrong, only resolve. When he made a 6 or an 8 on a hole, you knew he had given his all to each and every shot. When the carnage was over, you could see in his expression and his body language that he intended to get back those strokes in however many holes were left in the round.

I'll always remember watching Jack play a tournament at the Lakes Golf Club in Sydney, Australia. He was trailing Arnie Palmer by five strokes going into the last three holes of the back nine of the third round of play. He hadn't made up much ground by the time he reached the sixteenth hole, and you could almost see him decide that time was running out and that he had better get on his horse.

The sixteenth at Lakes was a short par 4, only 350 yards, but a lake on the direct route to the green. The usual play was to the left toward a thin strip of fairway by a sand dune about 240 yards out, an easy pitch. But on this day Jack wasn't about to lay up. With a slight breeze behind him he hit a 3-wood that carried 298 yards over the water and onto the green. He holed the putt for a 2.

The next hole is a tough par 3, 195 yards uphill. Jack hit a 4-iron to about twelve feet and holed that putt as well. The eighteenth is a dogleg par 5 to the right, with a marsh running along the right side. You can cut off as much of the dogleg as you dare. Again with the breeze,

Jack hit an enormous drive—with a persimmon driver, don't forget—that carried about 290 yards in the air. He hit the green with a perfectly executed second and, sure enough, holed out for a 3. He finished eagle-birdie-eagle to go into the final round tied for the lead. He didn't play as well the next day, but that hardly mattered. The game he displayed on that stretch of three holes, with power, control and clutch putting, was simply out of this world.

I have also loved watching Lee Trevino, a master shot-maker with the heart of a hustler. It seemed that Lee never hit a straight shot. It was always a delicate fade, a bit of a draw, a little high, one shot a bit hard and the next on the softer side—whatever was called for at the moment. He's a truly imaginative and creative player.

It's interesting to look at Trevino's game next to that of Nick Faldo. Faldo had a magnificent run of championship golf, yet I've always thought he focused too much on swing mechanics and other theories of the game. This isn't to say that he didn't make that approach work. He was tremendously successful, of course, but comparing his game to Trevino's helps illustrate the time-honored adage about golf and those who play it—that you can tell a tremendous amount about people's character and personality by playing just one round of golf with them.

7

PHILOSOPHIZING

I do think it's accurate to say that golf can show how well-rounded someone's personality is. In my experience, I've discovered people who cheat at golf are likely to cheat in business, in politics, in life. And if they are honorable in golf, chances are you'll find that they are also honorable in other dimensions as well.

I played in a championship in Australia one year with a partner I knew pretty well, but not well enough, as it turned out. It was an alternate-shot format, meaning one player tees off on one hole, the partner tees off on the next, and so on. Often, to speed up play, the partner not driving on a hole will walk up ahead to prepare for the second shot, which will be his. On one hole I drove, I was fairly sure the ball had drifted off into the rough, but when I got to my ball I found it sitting pretty in the fairway. I expressed some surprise, but my partner said we had gotten a lucky bounce. One of our opponents seemed to be steaming, however, and told me the ball had been moved.

On my next turn to drive, I deliberately hit the ball far to the left into the long grass way off the fairway. There was no way to get a good enough bounce to put us back on the fairway. Our resulting score at the hole ended our chances in the tournament, which made me feel much better—especially later when that partner was caught cheating in another tournament.

Not to wax overly philosophical, but golf can be a great teacher. In golf as in life, things tend to even out if you wait long enough. Bobby Jones said, "Golf is the closest game to the game we call life. You get bad breaks from good shots; you get good breaks from bad shots—

but you have to play the ball where it lies."

Something Tom Watson once said also resonates with me and speaks to the notion of golf as a microcosm of life. Tom said that he went about winning by first learning how to lose, pointing out that he had won only once in every nine times he competed. His attitude says that patience breeds optimism, that things will turn all right if you stay focused and forthright— and keep working your tail off. That's been my belief also.

I have always tried to conduct business the way I play golf, and vice versa. In golf you always come across people who play mind games, trying to upset your concentration or otherwise behaving badly. I don't hesitate to confront such people, firmly but not aggressively. I like the competition to remain pure, whether in golf or in business. I never saw the merit of taking advantage of a vendor or competitor, for example. One way or another, that kind of behavior is almost certainly going to backfire.

The thing about golf is that it's so completely personal. It's about you and the ball. It's interesting that so many professional athletes in other sports adopt golf as their second sport. In team sports, they must depend on others for their success, whether through the strengths of their teammates or the weaknesses of their opponents. In golf, they can rely only on themselves. By its very nature, golf demands this.

In other ball sports, you are primarily reactive because your actions are externally initiated. Golf requires you to be proactive, to make things happen entirely of your own will. Perhaps that's why it has always attracted self-starters, people who are comfortable functioning on their own. That doesn't mean you have to be a loner. But it does mean that the qualities of self-reliance, patience, and perseverance that are nurtured on the golf course can and do carry over into all aspects of one's life, and almost always for the better.

I am immensely grateful to the game of golf. I don't know where I would have been without it. It has given me my place in the world and served as the foundation for my entire education as a human being, and in every way enriched my life.

PART II

COBRA GOLF
GETS ITS START

8

THE CALIFORNIA ADVANTAGE

It isn't entirely coincidental that Southern California became home to so many golf equipment manufacturers, either start-ups or established companies that moved there from other parts of the country. By the 1970s California had become the center of the American aerospace industry. At that time many industries were learning from and benefiting from technological advances that were coming out of aerospace work. Golf equipment was no exception.

The location was a good choice for the golf industry, not only because of the proximity to such a hotbed of research and development, but also because of the ease of access to burgeoning markets for golf equipment. From Los Angeles one can get to either Europe or Asia in roughly the same amount of time. As the golf equipment industry grew more international in scope, California made more and more sense as the place to be. It was as close as an American-based manufacturer was likely to get both to the exploding Japanese market and to Taiwan, where many of the most cost-effective producers of quality club heads and shafts were located.

Beyond these strategic concerns, southern California just naturally has a lot to offer. The weather is consistent, with temperatures generally in the seventies, abundant sunshine, and little wind. That's pleasant in and of itself, but for the golf industry it also allows for year-round testing of clubs and balls. It's no accident that millions of people from around the country and around the world have found their way to this sunny paradise.

Newer companies such as Callaway, Taylor Made, and Aldila started up business in the area in the 1970s and 1980s. One older established firm, Titleist, after it had bought the California-based Golfcraft Company, had its entire club-making facility located there. That such a large segment of the golf industry was now located in California also spoke to the game's evolution into a more modern phenomenon. From small, primitively equipped, stove-heated workshops in windswept Scotland, the major equipment manufacturing enterprise had now moved to brightly lit, computerized, air-conditioned plants on the warm, sun-drenched southwest coast of the United States.

9

BEGINNINGS

My own arrival in California from my native Australia, together with my wife and two children, took place in the fall of 1973. The lovely climate and landscape had the added advantage of reminding us of home.

I had spent my younger years in amateur golf, in golf equipment sales with the Dunlop Company in Melbourne, traveling worldwide on the pro tour with Peter Thomson, and working in design, sales and manufacture at Precision Golf Forging in Sydney. Now, with the help of a few very good friends, I was ready to fulfill the dream that had been gaining strength for years, of setting up my own golf equipment business.

My friend Bud Leach promptly made good on an earlier promise to put some money into my venture, and Carl Ross of the Lynx Company, among others, helped me tremendously. Also, as it happened, Bud had a building in Kearney Mesa where he was manufacturing racquetball racquets. Luckily for me there were 3,000 square feet of unused space in that building, just enough room for a small start-up company. That's where Cobra Golf began.

These were not ideal times to be getting a new business off the ground. In 1973 the economy was healthy enough, if not exactly vibrant. But the first major oil crisis hit in 1974, triggering a significant slump. The golf industry is not especially vulnerable to economic downturns, but I had set my sights on the Japanese market and Japan had been hard hit. However, having made the commitment, I was invested both financially and emotionally, and was not prepared to back off my plan.

I had designed a set of irons while still in Australia, and had brought the masters with me to California. The clubs incorporated everything I had learned about axis weighting from Bill Johnston, an outstanding artisan at Precision Golf Forging, along with some ideas of my own. They were to be my first product.

My intention was to use the lost-wax, or casting, process rather than the traditional forging of iron heads. Among the first commercial clubs produced with this process were Karsten Solheim's putters, and by now he was also making his set of cast irons, the Ping Eye model. These clubs had been an immediate hit in the marketplace and caught the attention of everyone in the business. No sooner had Solheim's Ping irons hit the stores than it seemed as though all his competitors were refocusing their efforts on the lost-wax casting method. In fact, his new technique had so simplified the process that many intrepid basement entrepreneurs were also inspired to try their hand at club making.

The lost-wax casting process can be traced back to antiquity. Civilizations such as the ancient Egyptians and Chinese used it to make jewelry and many other metal goods. Although it remains in use today for these purposes, the process can, oddly enough, be called high-tech when it comes to golf. Casting was introduced to golf equipment manufacture relatively recently and was adopted directly from the aerospace industry.

Cobra's first irons were cast by the man who actually originated the process in golf, Bob McClellan. McClellan operated Advanced Casting in Los Angeles and most of his work was for aerospace companies. Casting is ideal for the precision devices and equipment that aerospace requires because it allows for extremely fine and precise work to very close tolerances.

Forging, on the other hand, is done with what is called black steel—non-stainless steel with a high carbon content. Carbon, when heated to the point of liquefaction, pours like mud and oxidizes so that there are tiny pinholes in the surface of the final product. But the stainless steel used in casting pours more like milk when liquefied and results in a flawless product, suitable for such demanding uses as spacecraft parts.

When the aerospace industry slumped in the mid-1960s, McClellan had looked around for ways to keep his business afloat. Being a golf nut himself, he tinkered with casting irons through the lost-wax method and found that it worked quite well. He never produced his own line of clubs, but he did cast heads for several other manufacturers, including Cobra.

Karsten Solheim himself had been an engineer in the aerospace industry in California, and sensing the possibilities, had opened his own casting operation, Dolphin Casting in Phoenix, Arizona.

In terms of golf equipment manufacture, casting offers a number of significant advantages over forging. First, it is less expensive, in terms of both the tooling and the handwork required. When the head comes out of the mold, it is already close to finished. It has the scoring lines, or grooves, on the face, the hole in the neck for the shaft, the imprint of the club's number, the manufacturer's logo and other designations, and the overall design and weight distribution of the head itself.

There's no shaping, grinding, or filing left to be done. Just break open the mold, polish it up, attach a shaft and a grip, and the club is ready.

The consistency of the casting process is unparalleled. Cast a hundred 9-irons and each one will be virtually identical to all the others. There's no waste or inefficiency, and the variability that forging entails—because of its dependence on the grinder's eye and touch on the wheel—is completely eliminated. I was fortunate to be able to catch the first wave of neo-modern golf-equipment manufacture, and I rode it.

10

GETTING OFF
THE GROUND

The good fortune of coming into the golf equipment business just as cast clubs were taking off did not immediately carry over into the marketplace. My first Cobra irons did not exactly fly off the shelves. It takes time to establish a name, which I deemed very important, and the reputation to go with it.

A good company name has to be memorable and easy to symbolize visually. In short, it needs pizzazz. One ideal, to my mind, is the universally recognized Mercedes-Benz logo. It may well be intended to evoke a three-spoked wheel, but to me it always seems to be a star, signifying the highest quality. Mercedes hardly has to put their name on their products as long as that symbol is there.

That's what I envisioned, a strong and memorable logo, as well as a short, punchy name that would sound good when married to the word golf. For that, I began leafing through encyclopedias looking for ideas, and soon came across a picture of a cobra. The snake fit all my criteria, was certainly attention-getting, and could be fashioned into an eye-catching logo, as it was easily shaped into a smart-looking letter "S."

When I tried to register the name, I found it was already owned by a company called Burke Golf, a division of PGA Golf (now Tommy Armour). Happily, when I contacted them, Jim Butz was the executive who took my call and he couldn't have been kinder. "We haven't used the name. Why don't we assign it to you?" That kind of friendliness, typical in the industry in those days, helped my dream of Cobra Golf become a reality.

As an aside, I should mention that a bit later on, the

name caused me no end of aggravation in the Japanese market. We spent a solid seven years fighting a legal battle with the Yasimotos, a big retailing family in Tokyo for whom we had built golf clubs, over the ownership of the King Cobra name in Japan.

At first we made only irons, and we were doing all right, but not making any major inroads. The clubs were well-made and had the low center of gravity and cavity-back design that were just then becoming the standards, but in all other respects they were relatively traditional. This was a conscious part of my design, combining the best of the old with the best of the new.

The clubs had the kind of look that golfers had come to expect in the irons, but it's possible those classic lines actually worked against us in the early days. Karsten Solheim's Ping Eye irons were a radical departure from traditional club head design, commonly described at the time as resembling a set of pipe wrenches. But they played extremely well, and while the trendier golfers were actually intrigued by the look, even many normally fussy low-handicapped golfers learned to live with it.

My own irons incorporated all the latest technology, but looked like traditional clubs, and at that particular moment in time, perhaps, tradition was not in vogue. Ironically, it would eventually come back into style. As I write this, the latest Ping irons look much more conventional, a far cry from Solheim's original.

Cobra's slow going in the early days was also a function of one of my key decisions. I intended to sell my clubs only through pro shops at golf courses, called the green grass trade. I was determined not to sell them in discount stores, or in general sporting goods stores in shopping malls, or even on Main Street. I don't mean to disparage these outlets in any way, as I believe they are valuable and important to consumers and industry. At the time, though, my decision had to do with what is sometimes called perceived value. That is, some consumers tended to believe that goods available in discount outlets or general merchandise stores were somehow second rate. That may have been so in some cases, but the fact was that soon enough, as the business developed, discounters and other retailers began buying up club makers' excess inventory at the end of the season, often including their premium brands.

Nonetheless, the perception when I was starting out was that the stuff available off-course just wasn't as good. For sure, I was taking a chance by limiting our outlets. Discounters and off-course retailers inevitably sell clubs in much greater volume than the green-grass shops, but perception is everything when it comes to marketing. I was making a superior golf club and did not want to take the risk of cheapening its image in any way.

There were business setbacks, too, and times when it seemed the whole operation might collapse. For example, there was the time I recognized that we needed to begin producing woods as well as irons to flesh out our product line. I therefore arranged to get four-thousand persimmon heads from a company in South Korea. Why South Korea, one might ask, when states such as Tennessee and Arkansas were full of persimmon? The answer is that the big three American manufacturers—Wilson, MacGregor, and Spalding—

along with a handful of others, had first choice of the homegrown persimmon and were taking all the premium material. The growers and dealers were not about to risk alienating their biggest customers just to help a little start-up like us. Instead, they would just tell me there was nothing available.

I had heard that a man in South Korea was producing heads made from good persimmon grown in swampland there, so I tracked him down and ordered the heads. When they arrived I saw that indeed the wood was very good. The workmanship, however, left a lot to be desired. The drilling of the neck was awful. The neck of a wood, where the shaft goes into the club head, is about 3 inches long and must be drilled with absolute precision—and not necessarily down the apparent middle—so that the shaft aligns correctly with the sole and face. In the South Korean company, it seems, they were simply holding the club head by the neck and drilling down the middle.

Anyway, the heads arrived and luckily I decided to check through them before releasing any of the payment. I ended up going through all four-thousand heads that night in my garage and found only sixteen that were useable. I hadn't been required to put up a letter of credit for the South Korean company, so I was able to return the whole lot at no cost to me. But I was still in a fix; I was holding orders for woods that I couldn't fill.

The solution to that immediate problem ultimately resulted in our moving the plant, and this would have important advantages down the road. I knew a wood maker in Sorrento Valley named Easy Arispe. Easy did excellent work and was making woods for the Japanese market at the time. He had about 12,000 feet of work space and could only use half of it, and we made a deal that involved our renting out half the building. I was running out of space in Bud Leach's building anyway, despite the fact that by that time I had bought Bud out. In my 6,000 feet at the Sorrento Valley plant I put together my irons, while in the other 6,000 feet Easy made his woods for various companies, now including Cobra.

So, all of a sudden Cobra expanded for the first time, an unexpected but as it turned out a well-timed move for us.

11

SERENDIPITY

It wasn't long after this move that Cobra introduced the Baffler and things took quite a turn.

It may seem odd to think that a business that became as big as Cobra began its rise after what amounted to a few minutes of noodling around in my office. That kind of serendipity actually happens more often than people like to admit in business, and it was certainly true in my case. One day I was musing about the future direction of the business and was struck with a thought—a memory, actually—of a club we had made at Precision Golf. The General Manager, Ernest Kermeth, had developed the club for Eric Cremin.

Cremin was an Australian pro who, along with Peter Thomson, got the Asian Tour off the ground. He was a wonderful wood player, much better than with his long irons, and he wanted a wood designed especially to play out of the rough.

Ernie Kermeth designed a club with a very heavy metal sole plate attached to a laminated wooden head. The sole turned out to be too heavy for the design and the club kept breaking as centrifugal force drove the heavy soleplate forward in front of the rest of the head. To fix the problem, Ernie experimented with a molded plastic around the sole, and sure enough it worked beautifully. He called it the Little Slammer and it became a very successful utility club in Australia and throughout Asia.

As I was musing, I picked up one of the Little Slammers I had brought with me to America and idly gave it a few waggles, the way golfers sometimes do with clubs that are lying around. It was a great club and did indeed move smoothly through heavy grass and get the ball well out, but it had a sharp leading edge that would sometimes dig too deeply into the grass.

I myself had hit a lot of short pitches out of the rough with a sand iron, rather than a pitching wedge, because the sharp leading edge of the pitching wedge would sometimes get caught up in the heavy grass, just like the Little Slammer. But a sand iron, played from grass the same way you'd play from a bunker—striking the ground behind the ball—will not dig in. This is because the sand iron has bounce, that is, the flange or sole is angled in such a way that the leading edge is off the ground. The flange hits the ground first and the weight of the club carries under the ball to create a nice soft lob shot. It dawned on me that this was something I could develop as an improvement on the Little Slammer.

Just as Ernie had, I started with laminated wood. Lamination, or the plying together of several layers of wood, creates a whole that is stronger than any of the individual components and is able to carry considerably more weight than the beautiful but relatively fragile persimmon.

I then attached a thick metal plate, but at first found that it was too heavy, making the club out of balance. (A club maker must think not only about the overall weight of a club, but about how that weight is distributed. For the club to be effective, weight must be appropriately distributed along the entire length, from the grip through the shaft to the head.)

I began taking away mass from the heel and toe of

the sole plate in a process not unlike the one Ernie Kermeth used years before when he made heel-heavy irons for Peter Thomson. Then a funny thing happened as I was taking away the weight from the soleplate: two runners, or long narrow ridges, appeared, running from the face to the back of the head, one near the toe and one near the heel. The space in between these two runners was flat—and the runners were angled so that the leading edge of the club was off the ground, giving it bounce like a sand iron.

The development of the runners on this club was one of the lucky accidents that sometimes occur in the creative process. The runners gave the club a distinctive appearance, but much more importantly, they made the club far more effective than I had ever imagined. I called the club the Baffler and eventually got a patent. In short order it became Cobra's signature club, and just as it got golf balls up out of treacherous lies, it got Cobra Golf out of a moribund situation.

12

THE BAFFLER
TAKES OFF

I devised the name Baffler for my new club partly as a nod to the old nomenclature for golf clubs. Before the days of numbered clubs, there were the driver, the *brassie* (comparable to a 2-wood), the *spoon* (or 3-wood), and the *baffy*, which had roughly the loft of a 4-wood. My club had about twenty-three degrees of loft, more like a 7-wood, but I liked the play on words that Baffler made possible: "Tough shots out of deep grass baffling you? Get the Baffler."

What was wonderful about the new club was that it could do so much more than just play shots out of heavy grass lies. You could practically play off cement with it and still get the ball in the air. It really was baffling.

The early days out selling the new club were exciting and often fun. I remember one time when I actually did hit the ball off cement with it to generate interest. I was showing the line at a regional PGA of America merchandise show in Ohio. One evening I got to talking with a group of club pros out in the parking lot of the motel where we were staying. I pointed to a big Cadillac a few yards away and told the pros that with my Baffler I could knock the ball off the pavement and right over the car. Of course, they thought I was a bit crazy, but they told me, a little nervously, to go ahead. I dropped a ball on the pavement and thank goodness I put a good swing on it, sending it cleanly and smoothly over the car. The pros were impressed with this little feat of daring, I think, as much as with the club itself. I took some orders right then and there and pretty soon started taking more. A lot more.

There were other key moments along the way as the

Baffler gradually became one of the most popular utility clubs ever introduced. For instance, I used to play a lot of golf with Gene Littler, a great golfer who won a U.S. Open and happened to be a member at the La Jolla Country Club, where I also belonged. One Sunday morning, I hit three or four shots out of the rough with the Baffler, which got his attention. He complimented me, but I explained that the credit should go to the club, not me. Naturally, that got him wanting to try it, so after our round we went out to the practice tee and he hit the Baffler out of every kind of lie. I would half bury the ball, putting it in divots and telling him to hit the shots just as he would an explosion shot from a sand trap.

Gene was amazed by how well the club worked and said he would take one with him to the next U.S. Open, in Toledo. He did. Afterwards I must have received calls from forty or fifty tour pros asking for a Baffler. They had all seen Gene hitting his in both practice and competition and recognized that the club could come in handy for them as well.

I knew I was on to a good thing and began thinking about how to maximize the opportunity in front of me. In those days we couldn't yet afford major advertising. A single-page black-and-white ad in *Golf Digest*, for example, cost $8,000. However, I got hold of a trade publication called the *Red Book*, which listed the credit rating of every PGA club professional. The ratings ranged from D, the best, which meant a pro who was up to date with bills and thus entitled to a discount, to A, someone with a less than blue-ribbon reputation in the bill-paying department.

I made a list of five-hundred D-rated pros, spent an entire weekend tracking down their phone numbers, and then called each and every one of them personally. I told them that I was going to send them each a Baffler club, with my compliments, and all I asked was that they take it out and hit with it, either on the practice tee or on the course. Step on the ball, I told them, bury it in the dirt, and then play it like a bunker shot.

I had five-hundred clubs made up for the promotion and sent them out as promised. Within the next three months, we had sold eight-thousand Bafflers.

Then the club got *really* hot and production went into overdrive. We extended the line, adding a Tour Baffler and then a driver, as well as 3-wood and 5-wood Bafflers. We even created a set of irons based on the Baffler concept. All told, we sold about 2.5 million Baffler clubs over a four-year period. We had finally hit the jackpot.

13

A White Knight

Ironically, the exciting introduction of the Baffler coincided with rather desperate financial times for Cobra Golf. Even as things were beginning to take off, I was gasping for air, on the verge of going completely under. I may not even have known it at the time, but what I needed was a white knight, and at just the right moment one materialized in the form of Gary Biszantz. Gary and I were introduced by my friend John Schroeder and we had played a few rounds of golf together.

Gary had been an outstanding all-around athlete in his younger days and now owned Ford dealerships in Los Angeles and San Diego. During the time we spent together on the golf course, I had talked to Gary about my basic business philosophy. I explained how I wanted Cobra Golf to build great clubs and offer them to club pros at something less than a top price. I related it to the automobile business, telling Gary that I wanted to build and sell a BMW, not a Mercedes, and was convinced that the market was there.

That caught Gary's attention and he admitted that after years of selling Fords he would love the chance to "sell a BMW." Once again I learned that in life as with the golf swing, timing is everything. The U.S. auto business was also struggling, a result of the major oil crisis of 1977. The time was right for him to get into something new.

Gary listened carefully as I laid out Cobra's financial situation, and told me he was prepared to get involved, but only if I would undertake a radical restructuring of the business. He said he wouldn't get involved as long as Cobra was carrying a high level of debt. He needed to come in clean if he was going to successfully recreate the company.

Gary also told me that I would need to write all the company's shareholders and tell them that they were going to be paid 10 cents on the dollar and that Cobra as they knew it was shutting down. We would continue to make clubs, of course, but Gary believed strongly that our only chance of survival at that moment was to start over again as a new company.

Moreover, Gary said I would most likely never succeed on my own because I didn't understand the American banking system. Dealing with the banking system was to be his role, and he was well suited to it. Whereas I was more used to the somewhat kinder and gentler Australian banking system, he had been dealing with the American banking community for years through his car dealerships and was a seasoned negotiator. He would almost certainly be able to work out better terms on loans than I would have been able to get, and this became the basis of a new partnership. Gary would handle the business and finance and I would be left free to do what I did best—make clubs and build relationships with the golf pros and the wider golf community that would make up our market.

I began writing the letters to the original shareholders and this led to some interesting discoveries. One friend and early investor was a Sydney hotel keeper. When he got my letter, he informed me that he had sold his shares to Kerry Packer, the media mogul and one of Australia's wealthiest men. I knew Kerry through golf, but had no idea that he was involved in this way. When I phoned him and explained the situation, he could have been uncooperative and angry about the return on his investment. He could even have tried to take over control of the business. But on the contrary he showed himself to be a benevolent prince, telling me, "Tom, do what you have to do." Between us we owned 60 percent of Cobra, so the restructuring went ahead uncontested.

We started over with $100,000. Gary not only put in some of his own money, he rounded up a few trusted— and trusting—friends to join him. I put up the last of what I had brought from Australia.

Cobra was becoming a community of interesting individuals. John Schroeder invested a sizeable sum. Gary Vanderweghe, uncle of NBA star Kiki Vanderweghe, became an investor and took on our legal affairs. Art Schultz, who was Gary's CPA in the car business, came on to handle our books. Pat MacDougal and Robbie Hirsch headed up the production side. And there were other highly valued and dedicated employees in all areas of the company.

The last key piece of the puzzle at the time was an old friend of mine from my amateur golf days in Australia, pro golfer Bruce Devlin. Bruce was an active PGA Tour player, the only one out there using our equipment. I insisted to Gary that the exposure we got through Bruce was vital, so Gary devised a plan by which Bruce would take the money we owed him in the form of shares, which would constitute a 7-percent stake in the business. "The Devil," as he was nicknamed, agreed and it turned out to be quite an excellent decision for him.

The staffing of the company continued to take interesting

twists and turns. Gary had a good sense of people and was able to spot talent in unexpected places. For example, one morning he walked into a bank, where he was helped by a teller named Leslie McKenzie. He liked her style and asked her if she was happy working at the bank. She told him that, in fact, she hated it. Gary seized the opportunity, invited her to come work with us, and to this day, she works as his secretary. A woman named Betty Baldwin also came into our office, and eventually she became Betty Biszantz. Gary brought in Bill Farr, a CPA who played golf at Rancho Santa Fe, and Jewel LeCorbiere, whom we soon learned was truly a jewel of a human being. All these people became important members of the growing Cobra family.

I myself made an unexpected contribution to the team. My next-door neighbor in Point Loma was a retired Air Force colonel named Jack Fitzgerald. Jack, who had flown in the Berlin Airlift during World War II, had never let on that he was a talented and experienced golfer. He had won the forerunner of the San Diego Open years ago, before it became such an important event, and had played in a half-dozen British Amateurs. When Jack and I were introduced through our wives, we hit it off right away, and he came and sold clubs for us for five or six years.

Cobra Golf really was like a family in those days, a close-knit family with all that entails. Gary and I shared an office at the start. He was always on the phone badgering banks for money and dealing with suppliers, while I was constantly chatting up golf pros and jumping back into the plant to check on the club-making operation. Gary's personality was as different from mine as you could imagine, though in the end we complemented each other very well. Gary had a notoriously short fuse, while I was comparatively cool. His temper would get the better of him sometimes, but we could always clear the air and keep moving forward. More than a few times I had to smooth things over after Gary got his ire up, but the truth was that he cared deeply about the business and any temper he may have displayed was always in the service of the company.

Gary had the qualities of a great business leader. He was driven, yet also a great motivator of other people. He could get things started, and just as importantly, he could get things done. He was creative as well has having a great memory and an exceedingly quick and decisive mind. Gary had the heart of a trader, someone who might haggle with you over your last cent, but who would never steal it from you. Even in those moments when we were going at it toe to toe, he was a fascinating man for whom I have great affection and appreciation.

We made a good team and were able to weather crises that would have ruined less solid relationships. One time, when the Baffler was just beginning to make its run, one of the big discount retailers in Los Angeles sent us an order for eight-thousand of them. That was an enormous order and we needed the money, to say the least. I didn't like it, though, since it contradicted my business philosophy of selling only to green-grass club professionals. Gary eyed the order when I threw it on his desk, and asked me what I thought we should do. I told him my feeling was that we should stick to our guns and stay with the green-grass trade only. "Then send back the order and the check," Gary said.

That was a significant moment, not only because of the scary business decision we made, but because of the emotional commitment it represented. Even though I often kidded Gary about being a used-car salesman, he showed real class in that matter. We retained our good reputation in the eyes of our target customers, who somehow got wind of our decision.

Gary is now in the thoroughbred-horse business. He has over eighty horses racing out of Cobra Farms, in Lexington, Kentucky, under the black and gold that were our trademark colors. I am grateful for, though not at all surprised by, his loyalty to the brand.

14

NEW
VENTURES

One of our most important hires back in those early days was a young man named Mark McClure, who became our sales manager and quickly began making major contributions to our marketing strategies. It was again Gary who had spotted his intelligence and abilities when Mark was a ski instructor in Sun Valley, Idaho, teaching Gary's kids. He had also been an assistant golf pro at a club in Palm Desert.

Mark was behind what I believe was the first serious effort by a major golf equipment maker to produce a set of clubs designed specifically for women. Up until then, women were not given appropriate attention by the club makers. Women's clubs were, for the most part, little more than men's clubs with the shafts cut down. Sometimes these clubs had more flexible shafts, but the heads were the same as on men's clubs and overall the clubs were simply too heavy for the great majority of women.

Mark and I got the idea for a more gender-specific club while on a flight back from Japan. Our thinking was spurred by the resurgence of the graphite shaft. After it was introduced in the early 1970s, interest in the graphite shaft had fizzled quickly. The torque, or twisting, of the shaft during the swing made it difficult for most golfers to control their shots. Additionally, the quality of the shafts was extremely inconsistent. By 1980, however, these problems had been pretty well worked out through major improvements in engineering and production. The Japanese were especially taken with this latest development, the lightness of the graphite being particularly attractive to smaller people as it allowed a faster swing and more distance on shots. Of course, these characteristics would eventually appeal to golfers everywhere.

In Japan, Mark and I had been selling Cobra clubs fitted with graphite shafts. On that plane ride we realized that the new material offered women the same advantages that appealed to the Japanese. We decided to produce a line of women's clubs featuring graphite shafts as standard. As an additional lure, Mark came up with the idea of offering the shafts in three different colors, one of which he would change every year to keep pace with the latest fashion trends.

This little add-on feature may have actually put us in the vanguard of another golf trend. Up until that point, there was really no easy way to identify shafts made by one company as opposed to another; all shafts were either unpainted steel or graphite black. Nowadays, of course, we see shafts that carry the distinctive identifying colors of their manufacturer.

Our effort to provide women with a more comfortable and playable club was a great success. At one point, women's clubs actually constituted 30 percent of our business. In time, we applied the same basic principles to the senior men's market, making clubs that were longer than standard, giving the older male player similar advantages to what we had made available to women. We would go on to become the industry leaders in both the women's and senior niches of the golf market.

Mark had another idea for increasing our business, one that seems painfully obvious now, but which was revolutionary at the time—the demo set. Back then manufacturers were providing pro shops only with individual 5-irons for customers to try out. A shop might have a rack full of demo clubs, but they would all be 5-irons from different manufacturers. Mark didn't believe that a player could get an accurate feel for a set of clubs just by swinging a single iron on the practice tee. He wanted golfers to be able to test a complete set of woods and irons over a full round in actual course conditions.

We came up with a plan that would provide incentive for club pros to talk up our clubs. If they bought two sets of our clubs for sale in their shop, we would give them a demo set at half price. At the end of the season they could sell the demos for a tidy profit or return them to us for full credit. We asked only that they solicit feedback from the golfers who tried the clubs and that they share that feedback with us.

We knew enough about how golf is most often played to think that some customs could work to our benefit. All golf clubs have regular foursomes and when one member of the group shows up with some new equipment, whether it's a new wedge or putter or a whole new set of clubs, everyone in the group takes notice. If the person with the new equipment happens to play better that day, it actually works out well for everybody—the manufacturer and the club pro, as well as the lucky golfer—because the others in the group generally want to try the new clubs themselves.

Even if the golfer doesn't play any better that day, everyone's interest has been piqued and a little buzz gets generated. In our case it turned into quite a lot of buzz. At one point a few years later we had eight-thousand demo sets in pro shops around the country. Not only did the pros in our program do brilliantly, but Cobra began a terrific run that ultimately helped us break into the big time as club manufacturers.

15

HOME
FREE

Looking back on the early days of the new Cobra, I remember Gary telling me that we would know that we had made it, that we were home free, when we could show a profit for every month of the year. I heard something similar from Karsten Solheim. He had invited me to visit his plant in Phoenix, a massive 280,000-foot operation, compared to our measly 8,000 feet. Karsten's plant was fitted with the latest computers and machinery, while we were still working by more primitive means. I was in awe and told Karsten so, pointing out that not too long before, he had been selling putters out of his R.V. at tour events. I asked him how he knew he had really made it and—surprise—he said the same thing Gary had said: when he made a profit every month of the year.

Golf is a very seasonal business, especially for a company such as ours that dealt only with the green-grass trade. In the winter months the courses and clubs in the north and east are shut down and sales are virtually nonexistent. You always hope that sales in the southern sunshine states will make up for those winter doldrums.

Back when the Baffler was our mainstay, the club pros who had done well with it began to ask what else we carried. We were prepared. We had beautiful irons and attractive and well-made woods. As the Cobra name was now associated with innovation and quality, the entire line began to sell.

After two years in Sorrento Valley we needed more room and moved into 20,000 square feet of space in Oceanside. At the time we were worried that we could never make use of so much space, but within two years we needed yet more. With the help of Alan Blackmore, a friend of Gary Biszantz, we finally built our own plant—70,000 square feet of space—in Carlsbad, which was to become the epicenter of the industry. Cobra and Taylor Made were the first to move to Carlsbad, and then came Callaway and others.

Before long we had to build another 70,000-square-foot building next to the first one to accommodate all the business coming our way. In the short span of five years we went from 6,000 to 140,000 square feet of manufacturing space. It was dizzying.

Among those who sat at our board meetings was Greg Norman, though often Denny Phipps acted as representative when Greg couldn't make it himself. Greg Norman's association with Cobra was another major breakthrough for the company and like so many other events it had serendipitous origins.

In 1977 I had brought out an iron, intended for the high-level golfer, made of mild steel. It was cast, but with the softer black steel that is usually used in the forging process. We chrome-plated it, partly for appearance and partly for durability. I produced the club in response to a growing resistance among the better players to the harder steels that were used for cast clubs. They complained that they couldn't feel the ball with those clubs and couldn't play with the kind of touch that is a critical part of a top golfer's game. This generation of golfers had grown up playing not only with soft steel clubs, but with a ball whose natural balata cover made it much softer than the balls currently in use. The new club could provide this kind of feel. I called the model, simply, Mild Steel.

The next year I received a phone call out of the blue. "You don't know me," the fellow said. "My name is Greg Norman. I'm in England playing the tour, and I wonder if you might be interested in making up a set of your Mild Steel irons for me." Of course, he wasn't Greg Norman yet; he was just starting out.

The European Tour didn't get much media coverage in America in those days and I wasn't keeping very close tabs on it, but I did keep up with what was going on back home in Australia. I recognized Norman's name as the winner of a recent tournament there, and Norman confirmed that he was that same golfer. He told me that he had an opportunity to hit some balls with my Mild Steel irons and liked them a lot. I took his specs—swing weight, club length, lie angle, shaft flex, etc.—and made up a set and sent them off to him.

Eight or nine weeks went by before I heard from Norman again. He called to ask me to make up a back-up set, so I mused aloud that he must have been pleased with the first set. Greg told me that he had won four tournaments with them in seven weeks!

We were in no position to sign anyone to a player contract at the time. Greg continued to use our irons until he joined forces with Spalding, a relationship which lasted ten years. When that contract expired in 1990, I convinced Gary that we needed an international player on our team and that Norman fit the bill perfectly. Gary, with his eye always on the balance sheet, was hesitant. With the Baffler having set us up financially and the rest of our line doing so well, Cobra had become a $25 million company. Gary had reservations as to the influence Greg could bring to Cobra in the marketplace.

Bear in mind that Norman had by this time become an internationally known superstar and was going to be very expensive. But my instincts told me it was time for us to have a bag on the PGA Tour. We had no tour pro representing us then, which made our success that much more remarkable. Nonetheless, it's a given of this business that one of the surest ways to reach the average golfer with your product is to have a tour pro endorsing it.

Some of our competitors had huge staffs, including a lot of mid-level players. That didn't interest me much, since having all those players to pay each month seriously drives up the cost of your product. I felt that one marquee player, a bona fide celebrity golfer, would be enough, and in 1990 Greg Norman had that kind of star power. Moreover, Norman's stature and appeal were international, which was crucial for us given the level of our business activity in Japan and elsewhere. In addition to the nine tournaments he had won on the PGA Tour, he had a British Open victory to his credit and had won more than fifty tournaments in Europe, Australia, and Asia.

Gary continued to question the idea, but I kept hammering away at him, making the case that this kind of relationship and endorsement was the missing piece of the puzzle if Cobra was ever going to make the next big leap forward as a company. Finally, Gary relented and then typically, invested all his enthusiasm and negotiating expertise in making a deal.

We signed Greg to a representation contract, and a real bonus was giving him an opportunity to buy 12 percent of the company and become an equity partner in Cobra—Gary's idea. Greg agreed and put up $2.1 million of his own money. What amazed me was that he actually wrote out a personal check, unusual for a tour pro used to getting something for nothing. But Greg said he wanted to put his money where his mouth was, which reflected not only his high regard for our product, but also his strength of character. Even more fascinating was that the high-flying IMG (International Management Group), the powerhouse agency that handled Greg at the time, inexplicably declined Greg's offer of 50 percent of his action with Cobra. The magnitude of their miscalculation became clear six years later when we sold our company. Greg's share was worth a cool $47 million.

The impact of this kind of endorsement or association is often intangible. It's hard to point to a direct relationship between Greg Norman's playing our clubs and a specific upsurge in sales, but it's clear to me that his presence made a huge difference. He absolutely increased golfers' awareness of Cobra and without question our sales increased because of his endorsement.

In 1993 we signed another high-profile tour player, Hale Irwin, who had been playing with Wilson equipment for more than twenty years. Norman and Irwin were the perfect pair. Norman was one of the most successful and celebrated international players on the so-called *flat-belly* tour, and Irwin was about to turn fifty and become the leading player on the Senior PGA Tour. We had our bases covered. We completed our crew with Beth Daniel on the Ladies Tour.

I still marvel at how wonderful our timing was. Irwin was still playing on the main tour when he defeated Norman by a single stroke at the 1994 MCI Heritage Classic, played at Hilton Head Island. Golf companies usually have someone actually sit with a stopwatch and clock the number of minutes of free advertising they receive when one of their player representatives is among the leaders. Whenever a player goes for a club and the camera lingers on a shot of his bag with your logo emblazoned on it, and every time they zoom in for a close-up of a player wearing a hat or a shirt with your logo on it, that's incredibly powerful advertising for which the network cannot charge you. I don't think we literally clocked the minutes during that tournament, but I have no doubt that over that weekend in the spring of 1994 we got our money's worth, and more, from our contract with Norman and Irwin.

Actually, that 1994 MCI Heritage Classic proved the wisdom of our gamble in another way and made Gary Biszantz a true believer once and for all. Right after the tournament ended, the CBS commentator Gary McCord caught up with Hale for an interview. Of course, Hale was wearing his Cobra hat, but he surprised us all by saying that while he knew he wasn't supposed to endorse products on the air, he had to admit that the irons he had just won the tournament with were the best he had ever played. He said as much again in a later interview. The irons were our KC1 (for King Cobra) model.

16

TECHNOLOGY
MARCHES ON

Hale Irwin's comments about his Cobra clubs at the 1994 MCI Heritage Classic were all the more gratifying because those clubs were the first oversized irons to come on the market and to win. Oversized refers to the size of the club head, not the length of the shaft, and the concept dated back to the MacGregor putter with the massive head that Jack Nicklaus used to win the 1986 Masters. After that auspicious debut, MacGregor's chief research and development man, Clay Long, tried applying the same design principles to the driver.

Of course, any club head has only one true center of gravity, which means one true sweet spot on the face. With smaller conventional club heads, shots struck away from the sweet spot, toward either the toe or the heel, would lack both distance and accuracy. The rationale behind the larger head is that increasing the size creates more perimeter area around which weight can be distributed. This in turn will create a larger area around the true sweet spot where a hit will feel just as good and be just as effective. In short, perimeter weighting produces an acceptable result even when the ball is struck off center because the heel and toe areas of the club can carry more weight. The same holds true for the bottom of the head, meaning that a player can still get the ball up in the air even when the club doesn't quite catch it cleanly.

Many of the advances in equipment technology were developed in tandem. The late 1970s saw the first metal woods, which were at first small rather like today's No. 3 wood. Future oversized wood heads were made possible by the lost-wax casting process and by graphite shafts. As manufacturers learned how to pour the metal walls of the head thinner, they could increase the size without increasing the weight, and so maximize the effects of perimeter weighting without affecting balance of the club. The lighter shafts enabled club makers some increase in the weight in the head without increasing the overall weight of the club.

Although MacGregor's first oversized driver didn't really catch on, Callaway quickly brought out its initial entry in this new market, the Big Bertha, and this club absolutely took off. Before anyone knew it, manufacturers were racing to make oversized clubs with the same kind of zeal with which they rushed cast clubs out immediately after Karsten Solheim's Ping Eye irons hit the market. Six or seven companies, including Cobra, quickly got into oversized clubs, but we were the first to try the design with irons.

Greg Norman adopted our driver, but we didn't aggressively publicize that fact. They say that imitation is the sincerest form of flattery, and since Callaway's driver was so clearly the category leader at the time, we worried that by promoting our own club we'd only be calling more attention to the success of their club. Instead, we concentrated our efforts on our new irons, advertising them with the slogan, "If you like the oversized driver, you'll love our oversized irons." Since we were the first, we were able to dominate this sector of the market quickly. In three years we sold 650,000 sets of KC1, establishing us, finally, as a major player in our industry.

Actually, it wasn't only the oversized head that made

the KC1 sets so popular. They also came with graphite shafts, standard. (Hale Irwin's original set had steel shafts, which he later replaced with graphite.) That they played so well can be traced back to a fundamental lesson I had learned from Bill Johnston at Precision Golf Forging two decades earlier. Our competitors were creating oversized irons by lengthening the face, extending it out further from the hosel, a thickened vertical extension at the heel of the club head into which the shaft is fixed. This naturally caused more droop in the shaft and more torque, making the club harder to square up at impact and causing too many shots to veer off to the right. I had learned from Johnston that you need a heel-heavy club if you want the toe to square up, so what we did was to make the head taller, that is, larger from top to bottom rather than from heel to toe. Our club had perimeter weighting, a larger head with a larger sweet spot, and could still be counted on to hit the ball truly. It was an extremely forgiving club.

Women and senior men flocked enthusiastically to the KC1 club. These were already valued customers of ours, having first come to Cobra for graphite-shafted clubs tailored to their particular needs. We ended up owning those segments of the market for three seasons. The combination of the oversized head and the graphite shaft made the clubs tops in the market.

17

STAYING FOCUSED

Graphite shafts became so much a part of our operation that we bought a company that manufactured them and folded it into our business. What was at first a good idea didn't work out so well in the long run, though, because we weren't able to sell shafts to other club manufacturers the way an independent company could. The shaft business was ultimately sold by Fortune Brands after they bought out Cobra in 1996.

We took another ill-advised detour during this period when I tried adding golf balls to our line. This was particularly risky, since the golf ball market is dominated by heavy hitters such as Titleist and Spalding (the latter, which included the Hogan line, is now part of Callaway). Again, my thinking was to concentrate on the green-grass trade and bring out a *boutique* ball. Slazenger had done nicely with this strategy and I thought that with our good name in clubs we stood a good chance of taking away some of their market share.

I started by going to see my old friend, Haruo Onishi, the head of Dunlop. Onishi had lifted the Japanese Tour off the ground by acting as its primary sponsor. His parent company, Sumitomo Rubber, made Dunlop and Slazenger balls, and Haruo explained to me that they were experiencing complications in a number of areas, including European distribution and the ownership of marks that was restricting their sales in Asia. I caught his attention with my proposition to sell Sumitomo a percentage of Cobra and allow them to market their ball worldwide under the Cobra brand. Onishi presented the idea to his board, but it was turned down. Sumitomo, it turns out, was the distributor for my competitor, Ely Callaway, and he had friends on their board.

Even within Cobra the idea of going into the ball business was not unanimously supported. A number of our guys had their doubts and it didn't take me too long before the plan was reconsidered. I remember being at a party one evening and overhearing a snippet of conversation that instantly caught my attention. The man talking worked for Callaway and I confess I couldn't help eavesdropping. He was describing the cost of the ball they were planning to produce. Callaway had decided to make its own ball rather than subcontract it out to someone like Sumitomo, and estimated start-up costs were in the neighborhood of $200 million. The raw cost of each ball would be $1.30.

I quickly started doing calculations in my head, thinking that Titleist, for instance, wasn't spending nearly that much per ball, since they had long ago paid off their plant and equipment costs. I tried to figure how Callaway—or Cobra, for that matter—could ever beat them at that game. It dawned on me right there that in the brutal competition of the marketplace, we'd get slaughtered. Thus ended any ball-making scheme.

Neither did we get heavily into putters. We dabbled in them for a time, but again realized that wresting market share away from the entrenched leaders would be an uphill battle. At the time, Titleist's Bullseye putter was still in demand, and Ping's putters, which had been the original foundation of that company, were still very popular. We made the decision to stick to what we did best—what management gurus these days would call our core business—irons, metals, and wedges. (The original Baffler, it should be noted, had gone the way of all other wooden clubs when metal took over that market in the 1980s.)

As critical as our decision to focus on the green-grass trade was to our success, it certainly was not the beginning and end of our business philosophy. Just as importantly, we were consciously determined, almost from the beginning, to avoid the vicious cycle that automobile companies are in, forced to refresh their product line every year. A car company brings out new models annually, or, as often as not, a new version of an existing model with perhaps some slight cosmetic changes. It's an expensive way to do business. The costs of re-launching products every new model year are very high. On top of this, customers have wised up and tend to wait until the end of the year to buy that year's model at steep discounts, as the manufacturers and retailers clear out their inventory in anticipation of the new year's models.

Inventory, at least, was not an issue for us, as we worked very hard to accurately estimate our selling volume and make an appropriate amount of product so that we were never carrying a lot of excess inventory.

I don't believe in treating golf clubs like perishable goods. The right club can last some years. Perhaps that's unrealistic in today's market, and to be sure, legitimate improvements in design and materials do come along from time to time and justify changes in the product line. But I don't see why a well-made iron or wood can't satisfy a golfer for at least four years, and conceivably more, returning honest value for the investment. After that, it's reasonable to think that technology, or the golfer's skill, will have evolved sufficiently to warrant new equipment. I just don't like the idea of making our customers feel disadvantaged simply because they don't have the latest model, as if there were something wrong with the product we had already sold them.

This point has been proven in my experience. In 2001, five years after our company was purchased by Titleist, I was asked by the new owners to revitalize the product line. New models had been introduced since the sale by their research and development people, but they really weren't in keeping with the Cobra culture. I wanted to know what had happened to 650,000 sets of KC1 irons we had sold from 1994 to 1996, the two years just prior to the sale. I started by checking e-Bay and found only sixteen sets on offer there. Out of 650,000. I took that to mean that virtually all those clubs were still in use, unless they were sitting idle in people's garages. I felt vindicated in our decision not to mess with the line every year.

18

INDIVIDUALITY

I must say that even as Cobra grew larger and larger, we still maintained the family atmosphere that made working there so pleasurable and rewarding. We were a small, tightly knit group of people. There were no suffocating committee meetings with everybody cowering before the boss and afraid to put risky ideas on the table. There was no friction between the idea guys and the number crunchers, no endless pouring over computer printouts or slavish devotion to sales statistics. Make no mistake, we kept an eye focused on the details, but we encouraged a constant and open exchange of ideas. Any suggestion, from anybody, would get its fair consideration. If we talked it through and it survived our tough devil's advocate questioning, we would go with it. It was an exciting time and I believe a lot of good things came out of our freewheeling business culture.

Our experience with the Baffler, for example, had demonstrated how willing customers were to buy single clubs as opposed to complete sets. A single club—a driver, a wedge, a putter, or a utility club—is more of an impulse buy. It doesn't involve the kind of financial commitment that a complete set of irons or woods does.

Since the mid-1950s, most clubs had been available only in complete sets, 2 through pitching wedge if you bought irons, and driver through 4-wood in a set of woods. Customers would add only putters and sand wedges of their own choosing, since they didn't come in the sets. Perhaps golfers felt that playing with an oddly mixed set of clubs would hurt their game, or perhaps it's just that conformity was more the cultural norm then. Perhaps a little bit of both.

Whatever the case, things began to change in the late 1960s and 1970s when people—golfers included—started becoming less shy about expressing their individuality. The newest generation of tour pros got the revolution started. Most of them were under contract to club manufacturers and were required to carry a minimum number of that company's clubs in their bag, say eleven or twelve out of the fourteen. Generally they'd carry a full set of matched irons, but after that it was anything goes. A driver from one company, a 3-wood from another, a sand wedge from a third, and a putter from just about anywhere, as this is the club chosen most idiosyncratically. I can't claim that the Baffler started this trend, but there's no doubt that when so many of Gene Littler's contemporaries ordered the club after the 1979 U.S. Open, a door was opened.

Later we continued the trend by introducing the first three-wedge system, a set of wedges with stepped increases in loft—fifty-two, fifty-six, and sixty degrees. This spoke directly to the evolution of the game. With new technology making players so much longer off the tee, there was less need, if any, for 2-irons and 4-woods, yet at the same time much more call for shots to the green from the 120- to 130-yard range. More golfers were using their sand irons from the fairway and the rough instead of just the sand, and the availability of different lofts gave them more flexibility in their shot selection.

A new club, the "Rusty," was designed by Phil Rodgers. It was so named because we cast it from the softer black steel that gave golfers more feel, and we didn't plate it over in chrome. Not only did the club heads rust and discolor naturally, but we actually suggested that people soak them in salt water to help the process along. Golfers liked the well-used look in a club that's as personal to golfers as their putter and as important for a good score. More importantly, of course, Phil, who had himself been a master wedge player on the pro tour, had designed a club that was as playable as it was beautiful.

Don't get the idea that all our equipment ideas came from people like Greg, Hale, Phil and me, who were scratch golfers or better. We listened to and encouraged ideas from anyone, whether it was about design or the manufacturing process, whether or not they even played golf. And it's fair to say that our clubs were playable and forgiving for any level of golfer, which was one of the keys to our success.

Another of Cobra's innovations was the first long driver, a club with a 46-inch shaft, when for years the standard had been 43.5 inches. There was nothing particularly revolutionary about lengthening clubs. Three-irons hit the ball farther than 9-irons not only because of the lower degree of loft, but because the shaft is so much longer. A longer club produces a longer swing arc, which in turn produces more club head speed and therefore more distance, without the player having to swing any harder.

Distance, after all, has become the holy grail of golf. We intended the longer driver for the senior golfer who has reached a point in life when both strength and flexibility are diminished and swings are slowing down.

We thought that some extra yardage off the tee would take the pressure off second shots, which were getting longer and more challenging. Ironically, the club also became popular with younger players, who were seduced by the chance to hit really big drives.

Again, it was the advent of the lighter graphite shaft that made the long driver possible. A steel shaft of that length would have made the club too heavy to be practical for most golfers. At first we also made the club with a graphite head, but we didn't stick with that for long. It was hard to get graphite heads of dependable quality, and very shortly after we put out the graphite heads, Taylor Made introduced the metal head and completely revolutionized the industry. Lightweight and strong, metal had all the advantages of graphite, but was much easier to manufacture.

I called our first long driver the "Long Tom," after the famous French artillery piece used in World War I. Ely Callaway perhaps picked up on that idea when he brought out his "Big Bertha," named after the huge German gun of the same conflict. Ely used to come over to Cobra to pick our brains when he was first starting out and his only products were a Bobby Jones wedge and a putter with a steel shaft (later graphite) encased in wood, designed to look like hickory. I may have let him in on my thinking about the military name. *C'est la vie* in the world of business. Or in this case, *c'est la guerre.*

The Crow Family—Young Tom, (second from left) joined by his father, John, brother, Peter, mother, Irene, and brother, Mac, in 1942 at the family's home in Camberwell.

Ah Youth!—Tom at age 18 at the Kew Golf Club in Melbourne where his father gave him his first opportunity to play.

Out of the Sand—Tom mastering a difficult shot during his early years of competitive play.

The First—Tom's first Australian Amateur Championship was played in 1954 at the Royal Melbourne Golf Club. Tom is pictured here with Ray Howath coming off the 5th green. Tom won the third round 4/3.

The Young Commentator—Peter Thomson at the Victoria Golf Club where Tom (standing to Thomson's right) and Tony Charlton (with microphone) were doing the commentary in 1958.

Practice, Practice—Taking a few swings on the practice fairway at the Royal Melbourne
Golf Club before winning Australian Amateur Championship in 1961.

A Winning Shot—In the final of the Australian Amateur in 1961 when Tom played Eric Routley and won 3/2.

The Victor—Tom with the Australian Amateur Championship trophy at the Royal
Melbourne Golf Club in 1961.

A year to remember—Tom in 1961.

Team Spirit—The Australian Team for the 1962 Eisenhower Cup played at the Fuji Course in Kawana, Japan. From left: Phil Billings, Tom, Doug Bachli, and Kevin Donohue.

Australian Team at the Kingston Heath Golf Club for the Trans Tasman Matches in 1961. From left: Tom, John Hood, Eric Routley, the President of the Victorian Golf Association and Australian Team Captain, David Dickinson, Bob Stevens, Phil Billings and Vic Bulgin.

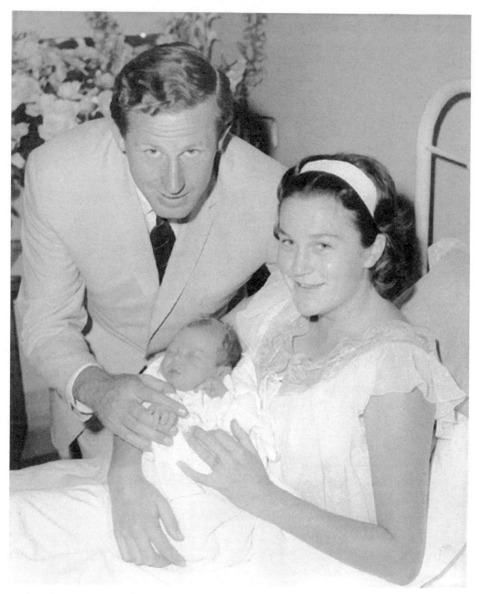

Another Golfer in the Family—Tom and his wife, Cally, welcomed their son, Jamie, into the world on February 27, 1962 in Melbourne.

Returning Home—Tom visited his mother, Irene, in Melbourne in 1976, sharing the early years of the Cobra success story.

Cobra Colleagues—Tom, Greg Norman, Gary Biszantz at Castle Pines Golf Club in 1990.

A Lifetime of Achievement—The Ernie Sabayrac Award

Tom and Cally at their Wyoming home.

19

ONWARD

By the early 1990s Cobra had grown large enough that if we had been a public company we would have been a likely target for a takeover. Remaining privately held had served our business strategy well. We didn't have stockholders or Wall Street to satisfy every quarter and every year, so we weren't under pressure to bring out new products season after season.

In our business, Callaway was the first to go public and to face that kind of pressure. It turned out to be a phenomenally successful move for them, and other companies followed suit, even Cobra. We hadn't planned on it, but in the end we had no choice.

In 1994 Cobra was a $100 million company—not bad for a company that made only golf clubs, with no balls, gloves, shoes, or clothing line. But we needed capital to keep up with the fast pace of our growth and, curiously, we were finding that banks were reluctant to lend us what we needed. Despite our outstanding record, the banks uniformly told us that the amount we were looking for was more than they were comfortable laying out for a company in our business. It's a funny thing about banks: it seems that when you don't need the money, they'll lend you whatever you want; when you do, they suddenly have a limit.

From his days in the car business, Gary was used to borrowing significant sums and he was frustrated by the banks' reluctance to back us now. The only way to fund the bigger facility we needed was either to find a financial partner or to go public. A potential partner did materialize when a group in San Jose offered us $100 million, but with some conditions attached. They insisted on keeping 30 percent of the money in the business, adding that if we continued to do well for two years they would take the company public.

Our little brain trust pondered that offer and quickly realized that if they were going to take the company public anyway, we could just as easily do it ourselves and reap the benefits. We planned an initial public offering, and took the opportunity to show appreciation to our customers, the club pros, and to our work force. In an IPO, the offering company has at its disposal about 5 to 7 percent of the stock to tender at the opening price to "Friends of the Company." We could offer that opportunity to our own close friends, but I suggested to the board that it was the club professionals who had gotten us to this point and I believed they should have a chance to participate. Everyone agreed and we offered shares to some thirty-two-hundred of our club professional customers. About twenty-three-hundred took us up on the offer. Of the nine-hundred who were for some reason unable to, at least eight-hundred-fifty wrote letters telling us how much they appreciated the opportunity, even though they could not take it up.

We made the same offer to our workers and lent money to those who wanted to participate but couldn't afford it. I like to think that this says a lot about the special, if not unique, employer-employee relationship in our company. I believe in the value, even the occasional necessity, of unions, but we never had one and it was never an issue at Cobra. We worked at treating our work force well, paying them well and rewarding talent and productivity. We provided assistance to employees with

131

personal problems and made sure they knew they had a safe place to return to once their problems were worked out. And we tried to create a genuinely congenial, supportive, and rewarding environment for employees and their families.

The IPO went wonderfully well. We had agreed with our underwriter to $22 per share. The opening bid was $32. Then it climbed to $66, we split it two for one, which lowered the share price, and then it went back up to $36. You can imagine how pleased those club pros were who had participated. Many of them sent us letters telling us about how the money paid for a child's college education, paid off the mortgage on their home, or enabled them to buy a new home.

Cobra was a public company for two years. Then American Brands, the parent company of Titleist, made an offer for 100 percent of our shares. They paid $36 per share, making our worth over $700 million. I will never forget the check I received for my portion, a check with seven zeroes on it. I stared at that for quite a long time.

After working so hard and pretty much having my way with club design for so many years, the aftermath of the sale to Titleist/American Brands was not easy for me, even though Titleist is the premier golf company in the world. They make excellent clubs and their chairman, Wally Uhlein, is an outstanding golf guy. He looks at the game through the eyes of a player and knows what good players want to see and feel in a club and ball.

Titleist targeted the pro and scratch-to-10-handicap amateur, while Cobra made clubs for the full spectrum of golfers. I was contracted to remain with the company, but was no longer in control of the product decisions, which left me feeling somewhat at sea.

When you sell, of course, you give over the decision-making authority. Cobra fell under the auspices of Titleist's research and development team, which was not a natural fit. We were asked to produce clubs that were similar to those already available on the market, a mandate which was antithetical to our long-standing culture of innovation. Cobra lost its originality, its particular personality, and our products were now the result of what I would call research and copy. We'd follow the latest trends, producing Cobra versions of whatever happened to be hot in the market.

I think what happened was that Titleist underestimated our stature in the green-grass market and the degree of loyalty and appreciation we had engendered with our innovative equipment. The sad result was that sales fell rather precipitously, from around $200 million in 1996 to under $50 million in 2001.

One hallmark of a well-run company is a willingness to recognize and acknowledge mistakes and change course appropriately. In the case of Cobra, that meant returning to what had always worked for us. In the winter of 2001 at the PGA Merchandising Show in Orlando, Florida, Wally Uhlein told me plainly that he needed me to revitalize the Cobra brand. He had been prompted by the declining sales and I believe, pressure from Norman Westley, the chairman of Fortune Brands. (American Brands had changed its name to dissociate itself from the tobacco industry.) I agreed, but this time I had my own conditions. I said I didn't want any of the Titleist research and development people involved and that I would take five of the guys from the early days of Cobra and go back to doing what we did best. Uhlein agreed.

It took us only seven months to get our first line finished and we debuted it at the 2002 PGA Merchandise Show, triggering a real comeback for the company. In that first year we did $115 million in business, and brought that up to around $150 million in 2003.

There were no marketing gimmicks involved; people just wanted what we were making again. In drivers alone, sold as a single club, we went from 2 percent of the market to 18 percent in 2002. Phil Rogers worked up a new line of wedges. And many of the club professionals have come back to Cobra with a renewed sense of excitement and loyalty to the company. They liked the look of our clubs again.

During the year of our revival, Cobra brought on a new general manager, Jeff Harmet. Jeff came to us from Wilson, where he had successfully taken the oversized tennis racquet to the top position in the market. Bright, perceptive, and hard-working, Jeff and his staff have been extremely instrumental in Cobra's return to prominence in the equipment market.

We know from experience that the last piece in the puzzle will be to sign a tour player. We have the clubs they can use, and it will only take one or two to come on board to validate our strategy and complete the resurgence of Cobra.

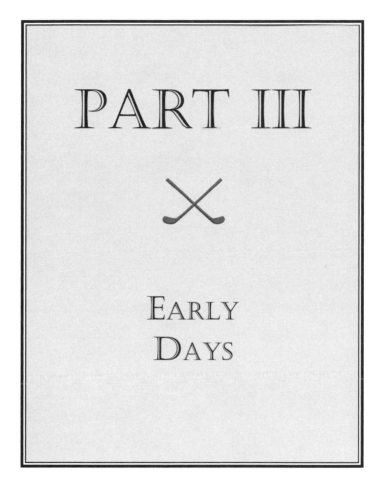

PART III

EARLY DAYS

20

SOME ADVICE ON
BUYING CLUBS

Not too surprisingly, I'm often asked for advice by people who are planning to go out and buy a new set of clubs. I'd like to say a few words on that topic here, for anyone who may be interested.

First, there are two different groups who are important: children who are just starting to play the game, and adults who already play and are wondering what to do when buying or upgrading their equipment.

Let's consider the children first. When introducing young persons to golf, it's best to start them out with just a couple of clubs because, after all, they first have to learn to make contact with the ball. I would recommend taking some time at this level. Give them a good chance to find out whether they enjoy the game and have some ability. Then, if it seems worthwhile going forward, the next step is to go to five or six clubs.

At this point, young golfers will need the help of a professional because now they'll need to get the right grip, stance, etc. The grip is one of the most important things in golf. A lot of kids don't progress as well as they otherwise might, simply because of their grip on the club. If you can start them off having a good grip, that's going to be a big advantage. A few lessons from a professional can make a real difference.

As young players grow and begin playing more often, that's the time to get them fitted for a set of clubs. There's a pride of ownership, I think—a feeling that they've earned their new clubs—that helps psychologically to take them forward in the game. Eventually, of course, as they continue to improve and to grow physically, they will need a new set of clubs that fits their size, weight, and swing. Fitting centers can be found all over the country, some fairly simple, some with sophisticated machinery. Titleist and Cobra fitting systems are very good, and there are roughly five-thousand professionals across America who use them and have been trained to fit people to the clubs that will work best for them.

When you're buying clubs as an adult, proper fit is definitely essential. You may already have played the game for some time; perhaps you've begun to feel you're at a point where you can do better than you have been. Getting fitted for new clubs makes a lot of sense.

With irons, a good fitting system will be very helpful in selecting the club type and shaft that will best suit you; I always advise people to invest the time to be properly fitted. As for the driver, this seems to be the most important club for most people because they like to hit it far off the tee. Take care to get the right one. It's wise not to let your ego get the better of you and purchase a driver with too little loft. You're really better off with too much loft than too little loft on the driver.

Unfortunately, the golf equipment market seems to have become rather like the auto market in that there's a whole array of new products every year. As I said earlier, I happen to disapprove of that business practice. My advice is that once you've got a set of clubs that suits you, stick with it as long as it works well for your game. It's fine to pick up, say, a new driver, an odd club, or a new wedge, but it's not a good idea to change your whole set on an annual or semiannual basis just for the sake of changing it or because something new looks interesting.

On the other hand, there are certainly times when a full-scale change or a major upgrade will be valuable. Again, this is true for young golfers who are growing and beginning to play better. Eventually, they will need to change to a set with a stiffer shaft than they would have had with their first set. Then, too, as we get older and begin to lose a bit of speed, that's a time when perhaps a slightly more flexible shaft is going to give us some help.

Another good reason to look for a different set of clubs might be if you're a slicer and find you're losing the ball consistently to the right. In that case, it might be wise to move to a more offset club. Manufacturers build offset into some clubs to help a golfer square the club more easily at impact. This feature can go a long way toward correcting your slice. Also, remember that there are plenty of opportunities to take a demo set out and play with it. I think that's a smart way to select a set of clubs because you can take some time to see, under real course conditions, whether the clubs feel right for you.

As a manufacturer, I've tried to create high quality clubs at an affordable price—a very high quality set of clubs, but not at the highest price—clubs that are designed for a substantial range of players at various skill levels, with the purpose of helping them to play better. Of course, there isn't one club that suits just anybody, or one model or manufacturer that suits everybody. There are nuances in design that help different types of players.

At the same time, club design should follow simple rules. Above all, it needs to be functional. The saying, "form follows function" is absolutely true in golf equipment. In other words, make it play well first, then improve how it looks. If you design the other way around, chances are you'll make a mistake. Certainly, it's equally true that when you're buying clubs you don't want to buy them for how they look, but for how they function.

The game of golf grabs you. You become fascinated with it. It's a game that's unique—and it's unique all the time, every day. Even if you played the same golf course day in and day out all year, that course would always present new challenges. So when you choose your equipment, look long and hard to find the clubs that will really work best for you, and that will help you to meet golf's challenges with increasing skill and enjoyment.

21

TURNING
POINTS

The Australian love of sports is known around the world and I was, in that way, a true Aussie. I grew up in Melbourne, where our family lived in a lovely neighborhood with excellent schools. I attended the same boy's public (in the British usage meaning private) school my father had, called Scotch College.

My older brothers, Mac and Peter, and I played just about any game there was to play. I captained the school cricket team and spent three years on the swimming team. And I was especially keen on football. This wasn't American football, or even the international game of soccer, but the rough-and-tumble game called Australian Rules football, which combines elements of rugby and Gaelic football. It's played over four 25-minute periods on fields approximately 200 yards long and 180 yards wide. With substitutions rare, players have to be in top condition, but even being in the best of shape can't always save you from serious injury.

It didn't save me. I remember going up for a ball during a match when I was still at school and coming down on the foot of an opposing player. He must have rolled against the backs of my knees and when my cleats caught in the turf I went over backwards. One knee was completely blown out and the other suffered serious damage to the ligaments and cartilage. The pain was indescribable.

Doctors couldn't surgically repair this kind of injury the way they can today, which is probably just as well. If they'd opened me up, I might have been left with a permanently stiff leg. As it was, I ended up much later in life with two artificial knees. In any event, I was lucky with the treatment I received. My father took me to the trainer of a local football club, a man named Ernie Saunders, who was able to put the cartilage back into place. I can still remember the popping sound it made. Amazingly, I managed to walk out of Ernie's training room. But although I was back on the field again in a couple of weeks, I had to accept the fact that my playing days were over unless I wanted to risk further serious injury. I doubt I would have ever played professionally, but I did love the game.

Not long afterward I decided I had to give up other contact sports as well, and even cricket—and therein lay a fortuitous circumstance. It was the football injury that ultimately sent me to the golf course, to the exclusion of all other games.

Golf had been one of the many sports that occupied our family, but it was not a high priority. My brother Peter was quite a good golfer and our father belonged to a club, the Woodlands Golf Club, but didn't play seriously. I had first played the game at age fourteen on a little nine-hole course called Wattle Park, about half an hour from our house by tram. Peter asked me along one day, and having nothing better to do at the time, I went with him. So began a career I could never have foreseen.

I recall that the clubs I used that day were a rather motley assortment, some right handed and some left. The mix didn't bother me because I was somewhat ambidextrous and actually played a few sports as a lefty. I probably would have written left-handed, but when I was growing up, the old superstitions about left-handedness being a sign of evil still persisted, and in my school picking up a pen with your left hand would earn you a sharp rap across the knuckles. Whether it was a result of that training or the lack of availability of left-handed clubs, I ended up playing golf exclusively as a right-hander.

I enjoyed golf from the beginning. This may have had something to do with the fact that I soon discovered I was pretty good at it. The game seemed to come reasonably easily. I never had a big slice, nor did I top the ball a lot, so I was never frustrated by the most common beginner's problems. I was able to get the ball into the air naturally, and even early on was able to control its flight pretty well.

And there was something else that appealed to me about golf: I could play it on my own and according to my own schedule. I probably should have recognized that this enjoyment came from the same streak of independence that would make it hard for me to be tied down to a conventionally sedentary career. That independent streak is, I think, a big part of what people call the entrepreneurial spirit, which certainly was a part of me and contributed to my success later on.

I loved the idea that whenever I wanted to play golf I could just hop on the tram up to Wattle Park and take myself out for a round. No teammates or opponents were needed. Even now, one of my greatest pleasures is to slip out to the golf course at the end of the day and play a few holes as a single. I can try some shots from the same spot and tinker with my swing. I love the way the late-afternoon shadows highlight the undulations in the course that you can't see in the midday sun, or that you don't focus on when you're playing in a group. I love the quiet time alone to clear my head and gain perspective on my life.

The Christmas holiday season in Australia comes in high summer and our family spent most of the time between early December and early February at a rented house in the seaside town of Sorrento, a place my mother and father enjoyed very much. There my father would play his occasional rounds of golf and my brothers and I would often join him.

An important annual amateur tournament was held in Sorrento on the last weekend of January, Australia Day weekend. The top amateurs in the state always played this tournament, and when I was still in my early teens and not ready to enter the competition, I would work as a caddy. This was not only great fun, but it also gave me a chance to watch up close some of the best players in Australia. I was the kind of athlete who learns best by watching and imitating others, and luckily I was still too young to have developed any really bad swing habits or have cluttered my mind with theories of golf mechanics. I can't measure how much my technique benefited from this early exposure to so many talented players.

My approach to golf has always been primarily instinctive. I've always played more by feel, and by my own sense of what works and what doesn't, than by relying on complicated swing theories. To me, it seems important to be in tune with the subtle changes in our bodies and abilities from day to day. A specific mechanical theory or swing may work well for someone on one day, but then may be entirely useless the next. The great Ben Hogan once said that golf is a game of constant adaptation, and that's how I see it, too.

Of course, I did get some formal instruction along the way. I used to hit balls with a friend, Bill Edgar, on a football field near his house. Bill had a great eye for technique and could spot fundamental problems. He gave me some very helpful advice.

Later, after I had become a scratch golfer, I got invaluable help from Norman Von Nida, something of an institution in Australian golf. Von, as the compact man in the jaunty beret is known in Australia, was probably our top player in the years immediately after World War II. He was an extraordinary bunker player, the best I've ever seen. He could handle uphillers, downhillers, sidehillers, and balls plugged deeply in the sand. In fact, the tougher the shot, the more Von seemed to shine.

I remember a time shortly after the war when four well-known American pros—Jimmy Demaret, Ed "Porky" Oliver, Jim Turnesa, and Lloyd Mangrum—came to play some exhibitions matches in Australia. They played against our best: Peter Thomson, Kel Nagle, Ossie Pickworth, and Von. I attended one of the matches at the Huntingdale Golf Club in Melbourne. After the match the Americans gave a clinic for the gallery, emceed by Jimmy Demaret, who was almost as good a showman as he was a player. After the various Americans demonstrated their respective fortes— Mangrum with the driver, Turnesa the long irons, Demaret the middle irons, and Oliver the short game—

Demaret told the crowd that they would be treated to a show by the best bunker player he'd ever seen, our own Norman Von Nida. Von put on an amazing display.

Overall, Von was just a great shot-maker, able to hit the ball high or low, or turn it in whatever way the situation demanded. The key thing about him, and the aspect of his play and his teaching from which I learned the most, was that he didn't go in for detailed swing analysis or worry much about weight shift or arm position. For him, what mattered was to develop a relaxed, smooth swing. In fact, he'd probably say that the more your head is filled with mechanics, the more you're breaking down each element of the swing, the less likely you are to be successful. Von often said that if you want to hit the ball farther with your driver, just tee it up a bit higher and concentrate on a nice, long swing. The longer your backswing, the farther you'll hit it, and vice versa. Too much thinking will mess up your tempo.

His relaxed swings notwithstanding, Von was a tough taskmaster with his students. He taught two of the best Australian touring pros of the 1950s and 1960s, Bruce Devlin and Bruce Crampton. Both became very successful on the American PGA Tour. Von would send Devlin and Crampton into a particular greenside bunker, on the par-3 third hole at the old Lakes Club, which presented a difficult shot from eight feet below the green. He wouldn't let them out of that bunker until they had holed at least two balls from it. Needless to say, both men became excellent bunker players.

Von was tough in other ways, too. Once he got into an argument with a 6-foot-4 American golfer, E. J.

"Dutch" Harrison. Unable to contain his anger, Von, who was no bigger than a jockey, jumped into the air and hit the towering Harrison in the mouth. Indeed, he was an Aussie classic, and I'm glad to have known him.

As I've said, Australians love their sports. Moreover, they have always been eager to support youths who show talent and potential. I benefited greatly from this generosity. Having shown myself to be a pretty good golfer by the age of seventeen, I was offered a junior membership in the Kew Golf Club in Melbourne. This gave me a place to play and practice regularly without having to fight the crowds on the public courses. More importantly, it gave me the chance to compete against some very good players who were among the club's members.

Having come into the club with a reputation as a good player, I was invited one Saturday morning to play with two of its best players. I suppose they wanted to check me out, to see for themselves how I stacked up. I didn't have an official handicap, and after shooting a 74 in that first round was told, "You're a four, Crow." There was no entering of scores into a computerized system as there is today. They just looked at my game and told me I was a four. I didn't mind at all. I was just delighted to be able to play regularly with top players, which is a sure way to bring up the level of one's own game.

In 1952 I played my first important golf tournament, the Victoria Closed Championship. The tournament was closed to all but those who lived in the state of Victoria, but open in the sense that both amateurs and professionals were allowed to enter. It so happened that Victoria boasted many excellent players, so the level of competition was quite high. Luckily, the tournament was played at Kew Golf Club, and amazingly, I won it, beating out not just local amateurs, but some top pros as well.

The win raised my standing quite a bit and I received invitations to join a number of other clubs. Two years later, after I had done well in several events, I was invited to join both Kingston Heath Golf Club and the Royal Melbourne Golf Club, prestigious clubs with wonderful layouts. Melbourne's sand belt was renowned around the world. I generally played Saturdays at Kingston Heath and Sundays at Royal Melbourne, a pretty fair double-header in anybody's book.

I felt privileged as a golfer, but I also came to realize that these memberships were important to me in other ways. Conventional wisdom has it that many a business deal is made on the golf course. Though I never actually concluded any agreements while standing in a bunker or marking my ball on a green, the connections I made in these well-regarded clubs undoubtedly opened up many opportunities for me later on when I entered the world of business.

22

A FORK IN THE ROAD

When I left school in 1950 I had taken some courses in chemistry and biology at the behest of one my uncles, who hoped I might follow him into his chosen profession as a doctor. I figured out soon enough that this wasn't really the direction I wanted my life to take, and so ended my formal education. At the time I was still young and somewhat without direction. All I knew was that I didn't want to be tied to a desk or follow a routine that was thrust upon me.

My father never pressured any of his sons to go into his business, although my brothers did ultimately take positions in the factory he owned, which made porcelain insulators. It's not that I wasn't interested by the lab where they mixed the materials or the kilns where they fired the insulators. In fact, when I later got into golf-equipment manufacturing, I was able to make use of the knowledge and experience I picked up there. But I think my father sized me up pretty accurately and didn't think that kind of work was in my nature. He recognized that something in me needed to be outside in the sun, not cooped up in an office or on a factory floor.

By the early 1950s, as my golf game continued to improve and I entered more tournaments, I needed to start thinking seriously about whether or not to turn professional as a golfer. It was not an easy decision. There is something undeniably alluring about the life of a pro golfer, at least on the surface.

However, there were more than a few reasons to think twice before taking that step. To begin with, there wasn't a great deal of money in it in those years. The professional tour in Australia was not yet well developed and while the American tour was beginning to catch on, the purses were still relatively small. The European tour had not developed much at all. Besides, travel to either Europe or America from Australia was costly and difficult. A golf professional would have had to have a club job in order to make ends meet, and that would have cramped the style of someone like me, who wanted to be out in the world, playing tournaments and meeting people.

Peter Thomson, the premier Australian golfer of the time, also dissuaded me from turning pro—albeit unwittingly. I knew Peter's game very well and realized that I wasn't likely to beat him out of much. As long as he was in a tournament, first place was likely to be his and very little would be left over, given the skimpy purses of that era.

Perhaps it seems clearer now in retrospect, but I wonder if, despite my desire for an independent and footloose lifestyle, I also somehow sensed that the life of a touring pro wasn't all it was cracked up to be. As adventurous as I thought I was, I didn't much fancy the notion of living out of a suitcase or finding myself in a new hotel in a new city every week. It's a nomadic existence, and in fact a potentially dreary routine in which golf becomes, in the end, just a job, and a hard one at that.

People fantasize about playing golf every day, earning a living at something they love. In reality, golf pros play much more golf than anyone thinks. College golfers, when they arrive on the pro tour, are generally stunned by how much they have to play and practice.

You play a round almost every day, which takes up to five hours; you spend four hours a day on the practice range, and most of the remainder is taken up with eating and sleeping and just keeping your life in order. A pro on the road, especially a young person in an unfamiliar city or foreign country, can feel somewhat unmoored in the few available idle hours, and the results can sometimes be very unfortunate.

Years later our family experienced this first hand through the trials of our son Jamie, who struggled with life on the tour. A brilliant golfer at the junior and college levels, Jamie played on the Asian tour and then the European tour, where alcohol helped ease the lonely grind of the road. Fifteen years ago Jamie wisely walked away from professional golf, though he plays competitively as an amateur, and has stayed healthy and happy ever since.

Finally, I just enjoyed the world of amateur golf. There was camaraderie between amateurs that one didn't find in the pros, who were, after all, competing against each other for their livelihood. Today, with the money in professional golf having become so big, even the player who finishes tenth for several weeks in a row can take home close to a million dollars. It makes it a little easier to buddy up to your rivals on the tour.

But there was something else that was keeping me from turning pro at that time. For lack of a better word, I'll call it the amateur ethic. It's difficult to articulate, but has to do with the honor and purity of competition for its own sake, for what might be called, simply, the love of the game. This intangible quality may be what appealed to me most about amateur golf. No golfer ever embodied this ideal more fully than the legendary Bobby Jones, and I have been greatly influenced by his example.

One aspect of amateur golf that I always liked was that most of the championships were decided at match-play rather than stroke-play. Simply put, stroke play means that the player who takes the fewest strokes over the designated number of holes wins. In match-play, the contest is decided by who wins the most holes. It's all about you versus your opponent. You can get a double-bogey on a hole, but if your opponent happens to score a triple-bogey, you win. Likewise, you can completely blow up on a hole and post an outrageously high number, but all you lose is that hole. Those strokes don't accumulate against you.

In a match-play tournament, you play one opponent at a time and if you lose you're out of the tournament. That's it. Stroke-play events, naturally, require a longer view. If you have a bad day, you're likely to have a chance to right your game and make up lost ground. But success depends entirely on your ability to manage your own game. There is none of the psychology—the poker-playing, the *showdown* quality—that comes with facing a single opponent in match-play. Match-play suited my personality and still does. I guess I enjoy the pressure and the interpersonal thrust and parry.

During those formative years of my early twenties, I was developing as an amateur golfer and also growing into adulthood, making my own way in the world. Most of my expenses were now my own responsibility. Earlier, when I was just out of school, having decided not to attend university I began to cast about for some means of employment. One ad I answered was for a sales position at something called the Hilton Hosiery Company. The interview went well enough, I suppose, and before I knew it I had been hired to sell women's hosiery to retail shops in and around Melbourne. It was a good situation for me, as it allowed me to continue playing a fairly heavy schedule of amateur golf tournaments all over Australia, and I stuck with the job for two and half years.

Then, in 1953, the combination of this experience and my growing reputation as a golfer landed me a sales position with the Dunlop Company. Dunlop is famous for tires, but the company also made a name for itself as a manufacturer and purveyor of sporting equipment and it had a large golf division.

Becoming a sales rep for Dunlop Golf in Melbourne seemed at the time not such a large step, but in fact it signaled my entrée into the business world of golf and set the direction for my career.

23

OUT IN
THE WORLD

By the summer of 1957, the great Australian golfer Peter Thomson had already won the British Open three times. It's hard to describe my excitement when I was invited to play a round of golf with him that year at the Victoria Golf Club in Melbourne. I had seen him play in the past, but had never met him, no less played with him. I was proud of the fact that I had gotten my handicap to a plus-1, but I was no match for Peter, who was a plus-5 at Victoria.

The day of our round, he showed up on the first tee with seven old hickory-shafted clubs, and yet declined my suggestion that he adjust his handicap based on this apparent disadvantage. He had never played with the clubs before; nonetheless, after working out the kinks over the first three holes, he shot a superb round of 68.

The golfing that day was terrific, but little did I know how important the meeting would turn out to be. Peter's attorney at the time, Peter Norris, was a good friend and golfing companion of mine and had engineered the meeting. Thomson was preparing to travel to America, where he was planning to play eleven PGA Tour events, including the Masters. After that, he would head to Europe for a number of events and, of course, the British Open. My friend suggested I accompany Peter as his personal assistant—what they called in those days a man Friday—looking after his travel arrangements, accommodations, and other necessary business. I was unmarried and felt I could leave my position with Dunlop, and I jumped at the opportunity. Looking back on it now, I realize that even though it was a job for me, I would have gladly paid for the experience.

As it turned out, this was to be a momentous, life-changing move. It opened up the world to me, both figuratively and literally.

In March 1958, Peter and I took a Pan Am Clipper across the Pacific to America, stopping over in Fiji and Hawaii. It was my first trip outside Australia and I was so excited that I barely noticed the two-and-a-half day ordeal that had made so many Australian golfers choose to stay close to home.

One of our stops was Louisville, Kentucky, where Peter was entered in the Kentucky Derby Open. It was one of the few times on that trip that I also played, though not particularly well. I missed the cut, as did another member of my threesome over the last two rounds, the great Tony Lema. Tony was just beginning what would become a very colorful, highly successful, but all too short career. What I remember most about Tony was that immediately after finishing the thirty-six holes we played that day, and having fallen out of the tournament, he headed straight to the practice range and hit balls for a solid four hours. I recall thinking that a player with such a naturally fluid and graceful swing, yet with such a powerful work ethic, was likely to go far. Indeed, Tony won the British Open in 1964 and was runner-up to Peter in 1965, but tragically died in a small plane crash in Indiana at the age of thirty-two.

Peter played amazingly well on that trip. At home in Australia and in Europe, he had played with the smaller golf ball that was still in use in Great Britain, but in America he was required to switch to the somewhat larger ball used there. He didn't win in America that year, but he finished in the money every week, and quite often in the top ten. It's my opinion that this terrific golfer has been underappreciated in the United States, and one of the knocks on him always was that he won all his championships playing with the smaller British ball, which in some situations is easier to play. I myself put no qualifiers on Peter's record.

Being the kind of young man who learned best by observing others, that time with Peter Thomson was invaluable to me. If my seasons spent caddying and watching top players at Sorrento were my elementary education, traveling with Peter was my post-graduate work. It wasn't so much the advanced golfing techniques I picked up from him, but more importantly what I learned about handling myself under pressure, adapting to varying conditions, and managing my game in a tournament situation.

A golfer on tour moves around a great deal, playing different kinds of courses in different cities from week to week, and sometimes even from one day to the next. To have any chance of success you've got to be flexible, adaptable, and able to adjust easily to constantly changing conditions and situations. One particular experience with Peter stands out as an illustration. After eleven weeks in America we were headed to England, where Peter was scheduled to play the Yorkshire Evening News tournament in Leeds. After spending eight hours sitting on a plane and six more driving from London to Leeds, a jet-lagged Peter was scheduled to tee off at 8:00 A.M. on the morning after our arrival. On top of that, this tournament would require him to switch back to the smaller British ball after months of playing the larger one in the States. His warm-up for the first round consisted of eight or nine practice shots with a wedge, about the same number with a 7-iron, and a few putts.

Peter had a surprisingly solid first round, which he used to readjust to the smaller ball, and in his second round he set a course record. The next day, he broke *that* record, equaled it in the fourth round, and won the tournament by a commanding fourteen strokes. It wasn't merely Peter's talent on display in this performance that stands out in my memory, but also his remarkable ability to adjust his mindset to whatever the situation required.

24

AMATEUR
YEARS

I'm certain that my success in competition over the next few years was aided by my having observing Peter play so closely and for so long. I learned just by keeping my eyes and ears open at all times, drinking in as much knowledge and experience as I could. I had won a few tournaments before traveling with Peter, but in the six years following that trip I had my most successful stretch in amateur competition. I won the Australian Amateur Championship in 1961 and was runner-up in 1964.

The victory in 1961 represents for me the highlight of my competitive career. Looking back on that week, it seems as though I never played better, though I know that no matter how well you're playing you also have to be at least a little lucky to win a major tournament—or indeed any tournament. But somehow, that time, when I came up against someone who was having a fantastic day, I managed to have a slightly better one.

I had participated in a lot of competitive golf in the run-up to the Amateur. The week before, I played in the Interstate Championships, representing Victoria, as I was still living in Melbourne (later, after moving to Sydney, I played for New South Wales). We were required to play two matches the first day, two the second day, and one the third day. That added up to ninety holes of golf, followed by thirty-six holes for the Australian Foursomes Championships. The Amateur entailed two qualifying rounds over two days. After qualifying sixty-four players for match-play, the first day of the tournament had a single match. Then came two rounds the second day, two more the next, and if you made it to the final, a thirty-six-hole match to decide the winner.

Quite an astonishing program—288 holes of golf in ten days time, assuming all the matches went the full eighteen. Not all of mine did. In fact, one of them, my quarter-final match, ended at the eleventh hole. That was my briefest match, but also in a way the most satisfying. My opponent was Stuart Jones, the great golfer from New Zealand. Stuart had won eight or nine New Zealand Amateur championships and had taken the New Zealand Open one year against the likes of Peter Thomson and Kel Nagle. Stuart and I were friends, but were nonetheless fiercely competitive with each other. Before the match, he had tried to psyche me out a little, telling me he was going to "wipe me clean." He played decently, shooting one under par for eleven holes, but I beat him soundly, 8/7. He never forgave me!

In any case, that was an enormous amount of golf to play in such a short period. Fortunately it was August, which is winter in Australia and so not as hot and grueling as it might have been. Still, I knew I had to maintain top physical condition and that year I had trained as I never had before. I ran four miles a day, and a friend of mine, John Griffith, who was a sprinter, showed me some excellent exercises to strengthen my legs and body.

I figured I was as fit as anyone could be at the start of this long stretch of competition, but I was also fit at the end of it, and this I owe to one friend in particular. This was a physician who was also a member of Royal Melbourne. We had become good friends, and he volunteered to caddy for me during these tournaments. He watched me closely. After a couple of rounds he pointed out that my weakest golf during any round would come from holes nine through thirteen. He suggested that my blood sugar began to run low at that point and that I needed some glucose in my system to bolster me. He began bringing along bananas, raisins, and other fruit that I would start to munch on at about the eighth hole. Over that ten-day stretch of golf, I lost sixteen pounds despite downing a big steak and two pints of beer every night for dinner. But the snacks sustained my energy during the matches. It was an important lesson for me in how to maintain physical fitness over the long haul.

Starting in the mid 1960s, we began to see many professional tour players reaching into their bags for some kind of sustenance during their rounds. Al Geiberger, the great American pro, got a lot of publicity for the peanut-butter sandwiches that became a staple of his mid-round diet. Steve Ballesteros would open up those little boxes of raisins, while other golfers put away apples and other sources of energy. It was but one sign of how golf was modernizing. When I came into the game, golfers did little or no fitness training. There was no weight training, flexibility routines, or cardio-vascular conditioning. Many golfers were more concerned with the good life than they were with proper nutrition and healthy lifestyles. Even the great Bobby Jones liked to relax in the evening with a glass of *corn*, as they called whiskey in Georgia. But times were beginning to change and these days the younger tour players are likely to be dedicated gym rats.

During my amateur years my horizons expanded

dramatically in both the level of competition and the geography covered. Among the highlights for me was being selected twice to play on Australia's Eisenhower Cup team, in 1962 and 1964. It's an honor, a privilege, and a rare thrill to play on a team representing your country in such a prestigious event.

The Eisenhower Cup match was instituted by a banding together of major golf associations around the world into the International Golf Association, formed shortly after the end of World War II. President Dwight Eisenhower, who was a great golf buff himself, lent his name to the matches with the intent that this kind of nonpolitical enterprise would help heal international relations in the post-war years and foster harmony among nations. The members of the association agreed that no nation could be barred from the competition on political grounds. For example, the United States was staunchly anti-Communist, but would not be allowed to veto, or even object to, the entry of a team from a Communist country, or a country with racial or other policies with which the U.S. did not agree.

A number of the teams in the Eisenhower Cup matches were from countries that lacked the kind of golf tradition one finds in America, England, or Australia, but nonetheless wanted to be a part of the tournament. It was a rich and rewarding experience for me to meet so many different kinds of people from so many unfamiliar cultures, and naturally it made for some interesting moments.

I recall one day, during a match held in Rome, when I was paired with a golfer from Malaysia and another from Iceland. It was a typical summer day for Italy, with high humidity and temperatures in the nineties, and the Icelander arrived dressed as he customarily would for a round of golf: heavy woolen pants, a flannel shirt, and golf shoes that looked quite a bit like hiking boots. By the seventh hole, the poor man was sweating profusely and looked as though he might collapse at any moment from the heat. When we reached the turn, I took an official aside and told him something had to be done before the man did himself in. The official understood the problem and I offered the Icelander a second set of lightweight clothes I had waiting in my locker. Such a gesture would normally be against the rules, but given the extreme circumstances it was allowed and the fellow was able to finish his round.

Another time, in Japan, we were introduced to our caddies in very formal ceremonies, complete with ritual bows and greetings. The caddies were all young women, wearing wide-brimmed straw hats tied under the chin with a wide sash, traditional loose-fitting pants, and wide-sleeved jackets. Their attire was a far cry from the tweedy Scottish tradition, to be sure, but these were excellent caddies who knew the game and quickly discerned the natures and temperaments of the golfers whose bags they were carrying.

I still chuckle remembering one moment from the first round, in which I was paired with players from Mexico and Germany. The player from Mexico had a beautiful swing and consistently struck the ball solidly, but he was having a horrendous time that day with his putting. In Japan, the greens are korai grass, which is very coarse and can take a while—a few years, even—to get used to. On the first hole the Mexican player hit his approach shot close to the hole for a good birdie chance, but 3-putted for a bogey. He did the same thing on the second hole, and again on the third. On the fourth hole, a par-5, he hit a wonderful drive and again another splendid approach in tight, creating an excellent opportunity for an eagle that could erase two of those bogeys. But again he missed the short putt.

Up until that moment he had kept his cool, showing no outward anger about his three-jacks, but now he was really steaming and he let go of his emotions. With the Bullseye putter in his hand, he angrily rapped himself in the middle of the forehead—and knocked himself out cold right there on the putting green.

Without missing a beat, his demure Japanese caddy reached into the sleeve of her jacket, pulled out some smelling salts, waved them under his nose, and revived him. I can only surmise that during the practice round the caddy figured out that the man was prone to fits of temper and had prepared for whatever might happen when the kettle blew. I suppose it was pretty rude of the German player and me to be laughing ourselves silly when the poor man came to, but we really couldn't contain ourselves. The story has a happy ending. Once the man was back on his feet, he actually began to putt better.

One of my fondest memories of Eisenhower Cup golf is the closing ceremony in Japan. The players were all seated in rows preparing for a group picture. On an impulse, I crossed my arms and took the hands of the fellows on either side of me, as is the Australian custom. Those players did the same with those next to them, and so it went down the line, and it grew into a gesture of good fellowship for everyone involved. It's a small thing, perhaps, but it symbolized for me, then and now, the true spirit of amateur golf.

Another Eisenhower Cup incident, in Rome, taught me that amateurism doesn't necessarily mean the same thing to all people. When I arrived there, the executive secretary of the United States Golf Association, Joe Dey, informed me that he did not consider me an amateur because I made my living selling golf equipment. Dey was something of a legendary figure in American golf. He held his post at the USGA for a very long time and was known to rule his domain with a ministerial manner. He had a reputation as a master of the rules of the game and a protector of the game's hallowed traditions. Among these was an arguably old-world definition of amateurism that dated back to Edwardian times, when it was considered crass to play any game for money, even as a professional.

Many people don't know that for many years, as late as the days of Walter Hagen, golf pros were looked down upon almost as journeyman tradesmen, and not even allowed to use the members' entrance of most golf clubs. By extension, it was unseemly for an amateur player to use the game in any way to enrich himself. Even someone who exploited his reputation as a golfer in order to make business connections could be considered a professional. Whether that was naivety or idealism is debatable, but in any event, it's fair to say those principles were regularly violated or ignored, and have long since fallen by the wayside.

At the time, I responded to Mr. Dey, "Mr. Bill Campbell, for example, who is on the American team, is an insurance man who almost certainly derives some of his income directly from golf," by which I meant to say that he must have used his reputation as a golfer to attract customers. Campbell was well known as a U.S. Amateur champion and Walker Cup team captain, among other golfing accomplishments. Though he didn't advertise these facts, he knew that people interested in golf would be more likely to listen to him pitch insurance if they knew about his competitive career, and there would be nothing inappropriate with his discussing that in passing. In my opinion, there is nothing wrong with this at all, and in no way does it diminish a player's amateur standing. There are hundreds of successful amateur golfers who use their name and reputation as a calling card in business.

To make a long story even longer, I finally told Joe Dey, "I will accept your statement that I am not an amateur if you will accept that anybody going to college on a golf scholarship is also not an amateur." Dey got absolutely red in the face and walked off. A few days later, having apparently simmered down, he asked me how I defined *amateur*. I told him simply, "Anyone who plays golf for prize money is a professional. Otherwise, you are not." At least he acknowledged that mine was an *interesting* way to look at things.

Even Bobby Jones once said to Jack Nicklaus, when Jack was deciding whether to turn pro or remain an amateur, "The right amateur in the right boardroom can make tons more money than any tour pros, and still bring a pure glory to golf." That may or may not be the case any longer, given the enormous purses available to the pros these days, but the remark does reveal Jones' savvy and his ability to change with the times.

Jones spent his entire playing career as a proud amateur, but after he retired he earned money writing and creating books and short films of golf instruction. Ironically, a few years later, when he went to play in the Masters—a tournament he himself originated at the club he founded, Augusta National—it was pointed out to him that he could no longer enter as an amateur. The USGA agreed to place him in a new classification: non-amateur.

My success during these amateur years may well have had something to do with the fact that during that time I married Carol-Ann Guest—Cally, to her family and friends. Cally and I had known each other since our school days and had stayed in touch for several years after school while we were both getting started in our own lives. I was absorbed by the world of golf, while Cally did a variety of things such as working in the Australian Consulate in Washington, D.C. Later she traveled for a year around Europe. We began seeing each other when she returned and after I had come home from my trips with Peter Thomson. Our formal courtship lasted only four months, and we were married in May 1961. This brown-haired beauty and I knew we were meant to be together. We still are.

My best playing years were between 1960 and 1965.

After that I quit playing competitively to concentrate on making a living and raising our two children, Jamie, born in 1962, and Annabelle, who arrived in 1964.

Moreover, during those same years I had been getting a real start on the career in golf manufacture that would become my life's work.

25

FATE PLAYS
A HAND

During my time with Peter Thomson I had been exposed to the world of golf-equipment manufacture in a serious way. Throughout our trips, Peter visited all the major American equipment manufacturers to look for better equipment, and also to learn what was new. The golf world at the time was dominated by the big three—Wilson, MacGregor and Spalding—and I was able to visit them all, tour their plants, and meet some of the legends in the business.

Among the men who made an impact on me during that time were Joe Wolf, the general manager of Wilson Golf; John St. Clair, a brilliant designer who created all of Spalding's clubs; the charming Bob Rickey, who ran MacGregor in those years; and Ernie Saybarac, a genius at golf marketing, who pioneered the way goods are displayed in modern pro shops.

What captivated me most of all was actually seeing golf clubs being made for the first time. There was some club manufacture in Australia, of course, but I hadn't paid attention to it during my youth, absorbed as I was in developing myself as a golfer. Back then, all I wanted was a well-balanced set in my bag and a convenient tee time. But the trip to America with Peter completely re-focused my attention and got me pointed toward my real future.

After Peter and I returned to Australia in 1959, I experienced another of those random, fortuitous events that can dramatically change our lives. It took the form of a phone call from Clair Higson, who owned a company called Precision Golf Forging, based in Sydney. Clair's company had been forging and assembling the Dunlop irons produced in Australia. I had gotten to know him while Peter Thomson was with Dunlop and Clair was making all his clubs.

Fate had played a rather strong part in Higson's life as well. Having served as an Army quartermaster during World War II, he decided, upon returning to civilian life, to go into the making of stainless steel cutlery, where he figured he had seen some opportunity. He brought over from Scotland two expert cutlers, Bill Johnston and David Fife, to oversee design and production. While they were getting the business set up, Higson learned that the two cutlers had also spent more than twenty years in Scotland forging golf clubs—irons.

Himself a keen golfer, Higson made an impulsive eleventh-hour decision to abandon the cutlery idea and try his hand at making golf clubs. He opened up shop in 1948 and soon was working with Dunlop. He also put out a line of irons under the name Precision Golf Forging.

When the relationship with Dunlop came to an end about the time Peter and I were back in Australia, Higson was looking for a way to make up for the lost business. He asked me if I'd be interested in opening up an office for him in Melbourne and working as a sales representative. The timing couldn't have been better for me and I took him up on the offer.

About a year and a half later I was made national sales manager and Cally and I moved to Sydney, where the plant was. This was my baptism by fire, as I was now fully immersed in the world of equipment manufacture.

26

LEARNING
THE ROPES

During my time at Precision Golf Forging, Bill Johnston was exceedingly generous with his knowledge and I quickly learned what a fine and gifted artisan he was. Because the forge was so overwhelmingly noisy, it only ran during the week, early in the morning and late in the day, when the plant was relatively empty of people. But the forge also operated on Saturday mornings, when most of the workers were off, and that's when I'd go down there and Bill would walk me through the process of making clubs.

It was on one of these Saturday mornings when Bill offered me one of the key ideas of fundamental club design, a mixture of physics and engineering that has stuck with me through the years.

On this day, Bill opened his right hand, spread his fingers wide, and wiggled his thumb, modeling the axis of the club at the hosel—the thickened vertical extension at the heel of the club head into which the shaft is fixed. He explained that the club needs to carry enough weight in that axis to compensate for the distance from there to the toe of the club head, about 3 inches. If the axis is too light, the shaft will twist too much both rotationally and downward during the swing.

Many golfers don't realize that the shaft not only flexes in the conventional manner during the swing, but also tips forward, or *droops*, in club-maker parlance. By beefing up the heel area of the club, one can minimize the droop and flex. If the axis is improperly weighted, the droop and flex will be such that the club head will rarely, if ever, square up correctly at impact. Most shots will go off to the right.

As I learned from Bill that day, the weight of the axis is concentrated in the hosel and the area immediately around the hosel. This is where club-makers make the fine adjustments that produce a properly balanced club. This simple truth of golf club construction has never, at least to my knowledge, been disproved.

Much later, in the post-modern era of golf manufacture, the first Callaway irons were revolutionary when they were introduced in that they had no hosel. Callaway's idea was that, by having the shaft connect directly into the club face, more of the mass could be concentrated behind the ball, in the impact zone.

However, in these early Callaway irons, there was not enough weight near the heel and shaft—at the axis point—to help turn the club face square at impact. Most shots tended to go right of the target. In their second generation of irons, Callaway began to correct this problem. They shortened the club head from toe to heel and eventually redistributed weight in the heel part of the cavity behind the head in order to beef up the axis area. The new irons were considerably more accurate, proving Bill Johnston dead right.

Bill knew his craft, and not because of formal physics or engineering education. Like that of many innovators, his knowledge was instinctive. My father, who owned and operated a company that manufactured ceramic insulators—where as a boy I had watched with such fascination what went on the labs and kilns—had that same intuitive grasp of complex processes and materials, and so I appreciated Bill's qualities all the more.

While at Precision Golf Forging I also learned a

tremendous amount from Ernie Kermeth, the brilliant design engineer. Ernie had a special knack for taking an abstract idea and putting it to concrete, practical use, and this is what he did with Bill Johnston's concept of the axis. Peter Thompson had asked Precision to make up a set of irons and had specified that he wanted to be able to contact the ball as close as possible to the axis without shanking it.

A shank is when you catch the ball on the inside of the hosel, sending it sharply off to the right, out of control. It is one of the most disastrous shots in golf, both practically and psychologically, and the source of much black humor among golfers. Peter's request amounted to another of those fascinating paradoxes of golf and golf history, such as hitting down on the ball to get it into the air, aiming right when you want the ball to go left, or playing a bigger ball because it makes the game more difficult to play in the wind.

Logic and instinct would seem to dictate that you should hit the ball squarely in the center of the club face, on the sweet spot. But in fact if you hit the ball closer to the shank, you'll have greater stability and less rotation of the club head. The point where the shaft meets the club head is the point of greatest stress when the ball is hit in full swing. This is what the great American golfer Bryon Nelson meant when he said that a shank is the closest you can come to hitting a perfect shot. I once got the chance to see Ben Hogan's irons, and sure enough, the ball marks on the club face were all between the middle of the face and the hosel.

Design has to be precise, of course. The heavier the

axis, the more likely you are to shank the ball, so finding the exactly correct distribution of weight in the club head is vital. Peter told us that he was looking for a very heavy feel in his irons, and at first he shanked every shot with the clubs we made for him. This was exactly where Peter wanted to start. From there, he asked Ernie to gradually remove weight in the hosel area, just until he got to the point where Peter didn't shank any more. At that point, the clubs would be perfect.

All great golfers know exactly where they are going to catch the ball on the club face with every swing. This foreknowledge is the reason Peter had such deft control of his ball on the course. As it happens, Peter himself knew a thing or two about the science behind all this, having studied chemical engineering.

My job with Precision Golf often took me outside Australia. I traveled extensively throughout Asia on business and met many interesting people, developing expertise that would stand me in very good stead when I was building my own business later on.

During this period I visited Singapore every three months or so, and one day was invited to play a round of golf with the prime minister, Lee Quan Yew, or Harry, as he was often called. Lee had recently been elected to office and later was to become someone I admired for his diplomatic and political skill. I accepted the invitation without hesitating.

I did not understand it at the time, but later learned about Lee's rise to power. During his campaign, he had led Singapore's Communists to believe that he was sympathetic to their cause, but after his election he actually jailed over a hundred of them, placing himself in a fairly dicey, if not dangerous, situation. Across the causeway in Indonesia, the leader, Sukarno, who actually did sympathize with Communists, was rumored to be plotting Lee's assassination.

Lee was riding in the limousine that arrived to pick me up for our game, which was to be played on a course called Changi. Changi had once been the site of a Japanese prisoner-of-war camp. Not surprisingly, we were surrounded by soldiers during our round—one company on the hole we were playing, one on the hole we had just played, and another patrolling the hole in front of us. We'd walk down the fairway between a phalanx of soldiers with their guns at the ready. I don't mind saying that I felt a little twitchy about the whole thing, but Lee remained calm and relaxed as could be.

It was terribly hot and humid, of course, and at the nineth green, the prime minister offered me a drink to cool me off. The big glass of thick black liquid that he handed me did not look very appealing, and I asked what it was. Lee acknowledged that it looked different and unfamiliar to someone like me, but suggested I judge with my palate rather then my eyes. The drink, made from specially prepared seaweed, turned out to be very nice and remarkably refreshing. Amazingly, I stopped perspiring and didn't start again until the twelfth hole, some half an hour later.

After the golf, the prime minister invited me to dinner, where my culinary adventures continued. The Chinese cuisine featured many animals and plants not normally eaten anywhere I had ever lived, but again,

Lee advised me to let my palate be my guide. The Chinese don't generally use charming or innocuous euphemisms to label dishes such as stir-fried stomach of dog or rat's ears, but I must say that I was again surprised and pleased by the food. This was something of an awakening for me, and ever since I have sampled the exotic foods of all the countries I have visited, and learned a great deal about international cuisine. Not bad for a chap who grew up on steak-and-kidney pie.

27

MAKING THE
LEAP AT LAST

In the 1960s, Precision Golf Forging was doing fairly well and was further stimulated to expand overseas by significant tax breaks that were offered by the Australian government.

At the time, the government was very interested in creating an export market for secondary manufacturing and was offering double tax deductions for companies that could establish overseas markets for Australian producers. You were allowed three years to establish the market, and then had to maintain it for three more in order to receive the deductions.

Clair Higson understood the opportunity and believed that Precision Golf could successfully export club heads, as well as fully assembled clubs, to Asia, Europe, and even America. He was right. Ultimately, export accounted for 40 percent of our overall business, taking me around Asia four times and a year and twice a year to America, where I would call on pro shops, manufacturers, retail sporting goods stores, and golf equipment outlets. I was completely and happily immersed in the golf business.

But by now, Clair Higson was getting up in years. Intending to leave money in his estate for his heirs, he decided to sell the company. He did so, to a man named Jack Chown, who controlled a mini-conglomerate that imported a wide variety of goods. Precision Golf became part of Chown Holdings, and soon enough an even larger company turned its eyes toward Chown. Jack Chown, who was also starting to think about retirement, sold. The company changed hands again after that, getting swallowed up by ever-larger sharks. I found myself spending more of my time in meetings and less of my time out in the world doing the kind of work I enjoyed. I was never cut out for corporate life, and the fact that I was getting less accomplished now than ever before made me uncomfortable.

A new idea had been percolating in my head for a while—the idea of starting my own business. In the course of my travels for Precision Golf I had seen how golf was suddenly booming throughout Asia. I sensed that the world market was expanding and that there was likely room for more club-makers and equipment manufacturers. I had, of course, done some of my thinking out loud, confiding in some of the friends I had made in the golf community. One of them, Bud Leach, was particularly important to me. Bud had been a champion water-skier in his youth and later an original investor in Aldila, the pioneer maker of graphite shafts that was based in San Diego. It was Bud who first suggested that America might be the best place to start my business. Given the circumstances, I was perfectly primed to take that suggestion seriously.

Inevitably, I walked into Clair Higson's office one day and told him that while I fully understood why he had sold the company, the new arrangement just wasn't my cup of tea. I asked him further what he would think if I broke away and tried to start something of my own. He asked me where I thought I might do that, and I responded, "America."

Clair was a wise and wonderful man, and without hesitating he told me, "You gotta try it." He explained that even though the market was rather small in

Australia, you still needed a large organization to succeed there. In America, he felt, one could be a local guy starting out on his own and still have a shot. The market there was so immense that a small operator could carve out a big enough piece to be successful without necessarily hurting the big companies. He asked me if I was ready to go, and I had to answer honestly that no, I wasn't at all, that in fact I had only just had the idea. He advised me, off the record, to hang on with Precision for a while, and when I was ready to go, to let him know. He made sure to say that the conversation was just between the two of us.

I kept my own counsel for nine months, and then finally I felt ready. My wife, Cally, had never been anything less than enthusiastic about my plan. When I first mentioned it, her only question was, "When do we leave?" I cautioned her that it wasn't going to be automatic, that we could go bust in a hurry, a lot more easily than we could strike it rich. Cally didn't mind, and her support meant a lot. She told me that if worse came to worse, we could always come home to Australia and get a job, but that she was ready to go. That's how Cally and I and our two children, ages eleven and nine, made the big leap to America.

And so began the real work of my life, the making of Cobra Golf.

POSTSCRIPT

BOBBY JONES-STROKE OF GENIUS
A Film and a Legacy

In April of 2003, as I walked the Masters, I was given an interesting proposition. I was asked to consider a role as consulting producer and investor in the making of *Bobby Jones-Stroke of Genius*, a major motion picture on the life of a true hero in the world of golf. The request came from my good friend Bob Keys of The Helixx Group and his partners, Paul Brooks and Jim Van Eerden.

The focus of the Helixx firm is to help its clients develop strategies that will accomplish life goals of excellence—something Helixx calls $Life^n$, or an *exceptional, unusual, remarkable, outstanding life*. Bobby Jones was a person who modeled that kind of excellence in his life.

I viewed this as an opportunity to complete the circle of my life in golf. I had accumulated a reasonable competitive record as an amateur player, achieved some measure of success in the golf business, and felt as though I had been able in a small way to contribute to the enjoyment of the game for players at all levels. Now I had the chance to help enrich the history of this ancient yet ever-young sport.

Through another Helixx client, film producer Rick Eldridge, I was introduced to producer Kim Dawson who had been working with the family of Bobby Jones for about twelve years to bring Jones' life to film. The life stewardship goals of each of us collided in a wonderful way, as we all came to share a passion to make an epic film about Bobby Jones. It would bc produced by a studio entity we would name $Life^n$ Productions.

Dawson had obtained the film rights to Bobby Jones' story from the family heirs. Dawson learned that the Jones family members cherished the memory of their father and grandfather and wanted to be sure that the film would be made with the utmost integrity, remaining faithful not only to the facts but to the spirit of Jones' life. We gave our all, every one of us, to telling the story well.

As soon as I became involved, I went to friends in Jackson Hole, Wyoming—Dick Johnston, Jim Eden, and Bob Jaycox—and suggested they join in the project, given that they all shared my admiration for Bobby Jones. The four of us (along with Bob Keys) put up a good portion of the anticipated budget of the film. For the balance, we sold shares to other individual investors, who participated for the prospects of a financial return as well as to create a philanthropic legacy and to participate in the experience of a lifetime.

We five principal investors have agreed that any profits we realize from the film will go directly to the charitable foundations we sponsor. Mine is the Cruffel Foundation. "Cruffel" is a Scottish word that means "as high as a crow can fly," and was the name of my grandfather's house in Melbourne.

In addition, there were pre-release screenings of the film held across the country which raised $3 million for charity, all efforts reflecting the spirit of Bobby Jones.

My role in the filmmaking process was to help the team avoid the kinds of mistakes one tends to see in golf movies. We knew that the first audience for this film would be people who play golf, many of them seriously.

Clearly they wouldn't abide any lack of realism or credibility when it came to golf swings, situations, language, customs, or manners.

Jones was unquestionably one of the greatest golfers ever to play the game, and he succeeded in that—in fact, he became something of a national treasure—without any self-aggrandizing hoopla. His demeanor was characterized by courtesy almost to a fault, intelligence without ostentation, and warmth and generosity of spirit. In a subtle but very powerful way he encouraged people, golfers or not, to do and to be their best.

He lives on through the Masters tournament that he and his partner, Cliff Roberts, originated, and through the club they built, Augusta National. Roberts was the mastermind behind the tournament, yet it's doubtful that it would have succeeded to the extent that it has without the imprint of Bobby Jones. The understated excellence that defined Bobby Jones has also become the hallmark of Augusta and of the Masters.

Jones died in 1971 at the age of sixty-nine. Sadly, current golfers and golf fans know only the legend, the historical personage. They haven't had the chance to learn about Bobby Jones himself, the inspirational and deeply humane individual. Even without golf, Jones would have been an extraordinary human being. He studied engineering at Emory University, took a master's degree in classics at Harvard University, attended law school, and passed the bar after only one year of study—all while simultaneously racking up his unsurpassed record of golfing victories. He spoke six languages and was fantastically well-read. An opera buff, he would hum arias to himself to calm his nerves in the thick of the fiercest competition. You can see young golfers today listening to music through their headphones as they practice, but something tells me they aren't listening to Verdi.

Bobby Jones began practicing law even as he was still playing competitive golf. He continued to make use of his engineering background when, after retiring from the tour, he worked with Spalding to develop a set of irons with the then-new steel shafts.

Perhaps most important of all, he was an adoring and devoted husband and father who believed his family to be the highest priority in his life. This is highlighted in the film by the only statement which is repeated: "There are finer things than winning championships."

Golf, of course, is an essential part of his story. Had Bobby Jones not been the great champion that he was, we probably wouldn't be talking about him today. But the real accomplishment of *Stroke of Genius* is its overriding emphasis on Jones as a complete, fully dimensional human being.

For the role of Bobby Jones as a youngster, we needed a boy who could not only act, but also swing a club well. We advertised in various cities around the country. In Atlanta, Jones' hometown, 280 boys showed up in one day to audition for the part. We photographed them, chatted with them to hear their voices and get a sense of their personalities, and had a look at their golf swings. We did the same thing in several other cities and were amazed by the number of kids who came to try out. We were even more amazed by how many of them had good golf swings. I remember one wonderful young lad in Indianapolis who arrived in period costume, complete with plus-fours and two-tone shoes. When we asked him to hit some balls, he said, "Do you want me to swing like Bobby Jones, or like me?" I have to say I got a good laugh out of that. The boy was self-confident and composed and had a good swing, but otherwise didn't quite fit the part. Ultimately we selected Devon Gearhart, and he did a splendid job with the role.

The young man we chose to play Jones at age fourteen was, fittingly enough, from Atlanta, and a good golfer. His name is Thomas "Bubba" Lewis. The first time he laid eyes on the Old Course at St. Andrews, he went out and shot an 82. I was impressed. Lewis' role is central to the movie, since Jones' teenage years are a significant part of the story. Jones played in his first U.S. Amateur at fourteen and impressed the gallery as much with his temper as with his swing. He was quite a hothead in his youth and even into his early twenties. The film poignantly details the process by which he quieted his tendency toward outbursts of temper.

Jim Caviezel gives a wonderful portrayal of the adult Bobby Jones. He had no real golf experience, but was confident in his athletic ability, having been a collegiate basketball player and triathlete. More than that, he has a rare intensity and a streak of perfectionism that enabled him to pick up on some of the emotions Jones himself had endured.

He felt sure he could master the shots he needed for the film and pointed out that he had learned to handle an epée in five days for his title role in *The Count of Monte Cristo*. One shot that he really did hit that made it into the film is the re-enactment of the famous bunker shot that Jones holed in the 1927 British Open. Jim made one good swing at the ball and that was all that was needed. No additional takes were necessary.

The need for authentic hickory-shafted golf clubs added another fascinating dimension to the process and brought us into contact with many interesting new people. There is actually a large group of golf collectors around the world and we were gratified by how many of them were happy to participate by making their clubs available to us. There's even a company in St. Andrews, called Heritage Golf, which makes this kind of equipment yet today.

Getting our hands on the costumes for about six-hundred extras was quite another matter, however. There are companies that specialize in this kind of thing, of course, but ours was a rather tall order. It was wonderful that Pringle of Scotland, which had made Jones' golf sweaters in the 1920s, actually volunteered to recreate these garments for us from the original designs.

Part of the human drama in Jones' story is in the tragic irony of the disease that struck him down. A vigorous and talented athlete, Jones spent a good part of his adult life battling a slowly debilitating and ultimately crippling neurological disorder called syringomyelia. Jones gradually lost control of his limbs and muscles until he was finally confined to a wheelchair. Often pressed about his condition, Jones was never known to complain, but instead insisted that we must all learn to "play the ball where it lies."

Lest I give the impression that the film whitewashes Jones or somehow depicts him in an unrealistically saintly manner, I should emphasize that the filmmakers worked hard to depict him as a real person, a fully rounded man, a man who enjoyed an occasional glass of whiskey, had a flair for colorful language, and possessed the kind of temper that left an indelible impression on people. In fact, some of that realism displeased a few of the men and women on the board that rates motion pictures. But the story would not have been complete without these elements, and they were presented in an even-handed, unvarnished, and tasteful manner. In the end, the film brought tears to the eyes of many of the Motion Picture Association of America's board members, who gave it a PG rating. The intention from the start was to produce a family picture, and that's exactly how it turned out.

The story of Bobby Jones is a legacy of historical and emotional permanence. My association with the film is an experience I will always treasure. People like to say that golf is the game of a lifetime. For me, *Bobby Jones-Stroke of Genius* has deepened the meaning of that expression.